LAW SAKES!

SCRAPS FROM A
LAWYER'S RAG BAG

*Dear Mrs. ...... Duncan
with grateful thanks for so
much help and encouragement.*

by

J. W. (Dick) Mackintosh

Dick Mackintosh.

Law Sakes!
Scraps from a Lawyer's Rag Bag

© J. W. (Dick) MacKintosh 1997.

First Published 1997.

I.S.B.N. 0-9531332-06

Printed by Highland News, 13 Henderson Road, Longman North, Inverness IV1 1SP.
Telephone: 01463 224444   Fax: 01463 235601

CONTENTS

PREFACE

It's all lies, just lies. But some bits might not be such big lies. Some might even be true. Assuredly, they all relate.

In case the true bits might ring some melancholy bells, I have submitted them to those who may care, with a question on publishing – "Do you say 'No,' or do you say 'Yes'?"

All said "Yes".

To dredge these stories from the depths of my subconscious has been to review some of the highlights of my excursions in law. And lowlights. Why did I write this book at all? Well, it was interesting. I wold say that. What about vanity? You tell me – Guilty, Not Proven, or Not Guilty;

I fear for your answer.

I thought the section on "The Fire," was too long for one chapter. Might be boring. So I split it up, and the six chapters are on pages 1, 7, 15, 27, 40, 51.

To

Syb

who was my inspiration.

All proceeds from the sale of this book will be donated to
The Highlands and Islands Tape Service for the Blind and Disabled.

THE FIRE (1)

"What the blazes is going on?"

I found his question both unintentionally appropriate, and unquestionably reasonable, but resented the ire.

The Laird Duncan, was known to me of old, and I did not expect kid glove treatment from him. In build, he was stocky. He was strong limbed, fair haired. In speech he was blunt in the extreme. So he was disliked by some without his being disturbed. I, probably more than most, was aware of his many acts of kindness performed furtively. I could forgive him a,lot. His accent was redolent of Eton, an establishment which he abominated. He was wealthy.

Cairncross estate which he owned, extended to two hundred acres arable, and a thousand hill, with a hundred acres of mixed conifers, and both banks of a modest river. He employed twenty men to work his interests in farming, forestry, stalking, grouse and pheasant shoots.

Immediately to the west of Cairncross lay the small estate of Drumcraig. To the west of Drumcraig ran the railway line, climbing southwards steeply to fifteen hundred feet. That caused the trouble.

South bound trains, passenger and freight, usually with two steam engines toiled up the incline, and in doing so discharged sparks in varying degrees of intensity on adjoining land. Surfacemen were entrusted with extinguishing these when a spread was threatened. Then cane the occasion when they lost control. Fanned by a fresh south westerly, the flames crept eastwards through the heath, over Drumcraig hill, and on a one mile front, to Duncan's land. The lush, tinder dry heather ignited the peat below, and crisis developed. A vast area of hill land lay at risk, plantations, dwelling houses, and fences, bridges, deer, grouse, pheasants.

Beaters were marshalled from estate, railway, and forestry staff. Vast Commission plantations were at hazard. Detachments of the Police, and of the army came too. The operation was controlled by units of the Fire Brigade, but beating was futile. Sunken peat fires resisted. The only method of limiting damage was by deep ploughing. The only complete answer was snow. For that there was a wait of four months.

"Have ye got a light Jock?"

RORY AND THE PLUMBER'S PIPES

He looked like Dopey out of Snow White, all four foot ten of him. Leaning slightly forward, he took tiny little steps, toes raised high, and feet landing straight - just like cartoon animation. Though thirty–five years of age, he appeared more like twelve, with that little grin he always wore, teeth clenched together, and look of complete contentment. The innocent blue eyes widened and eyebrows raised in concentration. His bonnet tilted over his left ear bobbed in unison, topping a dossan of fair hair, with little leggies never to straighten at the knee. Dress was conventional enough – trousers, and jacket always worn open in default of buttons, striped shirt secured by a brass stud at the neck. Bereft of his grin you would say he had a good strong head and chin. How wrong could you be. He was illiterate, but he could count money.

I should have known him. Most did – but then there was a nine year gap in my attention to local affairs, between swotting law and attending to Hitler.

Before Legal Aid, junior lawyers acted free as "Solicitors for the Poor," in rotation. I was so rotating when the Sheriff Clerk told me I had a client. That's when I met Rory, on a charge of theft.

There was no time to get the story before the Court convened, but he was certain of one thing – his plea had to be "Not Guilty." The charge related to the disappearance of copper and lead piping from a plumber's yard.

When Rory called upon me by appointment I had difficulty at first in understanding his mixture of English, Gaelic, and Cant. He was one of the travelling people. We tend to call them tinkers, but I spurn that term. It has pejorative connotations. Rory was first generation housed, but still took to the road in summer, when he specialised in the horse trade.

His story, told ever so earnestly, was that on the night in question he was playing cards with two friends until eleven p.m. and then went to bed.

He took me to meet his friends, also travelling people, and they confirmed. I went to see the plumber's yard, on three sides bounded by the walls of shops. The fourth side was guarded by an eight foot fence and a double gate, both of which had wooden spars extending above, another two feet. These spars were generously laced with barbed wire. I could not imagine even an enthusiastic intruder gaining access, except by opening the gate, which was not done.

I was beginning to think Rory might have a case, and called on the Procurator Fiscal to see if he would enlighten me further.

"You sure are wasting your time," said he. "Rory has a list of previous convictions as long as your arm. He ALWAYS PLEADS 'Not Guilty' and he is always convicted."

I went back to Rory and subjected him to a severe grilling. He wouldn't budge. He was "Not Guilty."

So we went to trial.

The Police gave formal evidence of their enquiries. The plumber identified his goods. A scrap merchant confirmed he had bought the stolen goods, but not from Rory. Another traveller admitted he had sold on behalf of Rory to the merchant, and split the price with Rory.

I saw my case going out of the window.

I put Rory in the witness box, for what it was worth, and he reasserted his innocence. Then the Fiscal had him.

I remember little of the stinging cross examination, except that when asked how he replied to numerous questions by the Police, Rory said –

"I just turned round and told them ... ..."

"I turned round and said ... ..."

"I turned round and just said again ... ..."

I had a vision of Rory whirling round like a catherine wheel.

Rory got one month, and gave me a cheery wave as he was led away. He had had his moment of glory.

Six weeks later he hailed me in Bridge Street. He quite liked the jile – good porridge and good soup, and it was warm. He tapped me for half a crown. His story was worth it.

"I just climbed a wee ladder on top of my barrow, and I threw an army coat over the wire. It was easy. There were boards on the inside of the door, so no bother getting out. It was two in the morning and not a hornie (policeman) in sight."

A year later I heard Rory was celebrating hogmanay in his favourite pub. He took a bet that he would drink a whole bottle of whisky at a sitting, and he won. But it killed him.

I include this addendum not as a funny, but just for the record. It made me real sad. He was such an engaging merchant when characters are becoming so rare. He may have been a rascal, but a benign one. I'm sure I was not alone in mourning Rory Williamson.

Rory aforesaid.

ALFRED – A SUDDEN DEATH

It was Agnes Fotheringham's voice on the telephone.

"I'm at Alfred's house. He's dead. You'd better get here quick."

The urgency in the voice prompted me to instruct my secretary to cancel all three appointments in my diary. I was at Alfred's house within fifteen minutes. There I found a Policeman guarding the front door, which was obviously clumsily forced. He accepted I had a right to enter.

Alfred, dressed only in pyjamas, was sitting on the floor, his back against the frame of the open door leading from the lounge to the kitchen, and chin on chest. The left leg was stretched on the floor exposed to the knee, and the right bent at the knee, foot flat down. Both feet were bare. The body was cold, the eyes open, and the flesh blue – cyanosis. Not a pleasant sight.

In his mid seventies, Alfred had been a widower for two years. He ran a small grocery business, which had been sold quite well, when he was seventy. He had had a drink problem in his fifties, which he conquered with his wife's help, and to my knowledge he had never touched spirits for twenty five years. He leaned heavily on his wife. When she died he was desolate. There was one child, Yvonne, on whom the parents doted. She was grown up and married to an insurance executive based in Canada. The son in law was a catholic, and Alfred did not like catholics. Being of an equable disposition, he made the best of it. So far as church going was concerned, to please his wife he practised, but he did not believe.

On the lounge coffee table there was a bottle of whisky half full with cork alongside, a glass, a see–through plastic bag containing about a pound weight of yellow tablets, aspirin size, and a scatter of old envelopes and scraps of paper.

On the first envelope I picked up was – "The pills were the ones Ruth had, and I kept over the years."

Ruth, his sister, died seven years before, and had worked in a private nursing home, though not in any way qualified.

Then there was a letter to his daughter – "Please forgive me for what I intend to do. I can't stand this lonely life any longer ... ..." It went on for four pages.

On another envelope – "I'm taking a terrible wallop of whisky to do this. I feel sorry for you."

And finally – "Goodbye. Forget me. No debt except milk and papers."

The words stood out and shouted at me – "I FEEL SORRY FOR YOU."

Had this something to do with her being a catholic? Don't the catholics take a pretty serious view of suicide? And Yvonne herself had two young children. What would the effect be of a suicide in the family? I made up my mind. I stuffed all the notes into my pocket, took the whisky glass to the kitchen, rinsed it and put it in a small cupboard with the bottle, washed the tablets down the toilet.

The Policeman told me the doctor had not called. I phoned Dr. Tim, whom I knew so well. He arrived in ten minutes, and I left him to his examination. He said I could collect the death certificate in the afternoon. I draped the corpse with a counterpane from a single bed, phoned the undertaker, and arranged with a joiner friend to come at once to secure the door.

Everything now depended on Dr. Tim. He was no fool. He probably knew what happened.

At the surgery, I ripped open the envelope handed me by the receptionist – and the primary cause of death – "Congestive cardiac failure." You are a topper, Tim!

I registered the death, and tried not to look too guilty. In the days which succeeded there was not a whisper of suicide. I may have done Yvonne a service. I doubt if the Law Society would have approved.

THE MAJOR – DIVORCEE

He looked every inch a Major – tall, straight backed, toothbrush moustache. He was a good natured chap, ready for a laugh, outgoing.

After the war he held a staff appointment in London, where inevitably he was much involved in party going. At a party following a theatre show he was introduced to a pretty young American actress, a lady bubbling over with the joys of life, intelligent with it, and a brilliant conversationalist. Her name was Vera.

The Major fell for her in a big way, and she returned the sentiments. The whirlwind courtship lasted only a month, and the subsequent engagement another. They were married, and blissfully happy.

But there came snags. The young lady, climbing the ladder in her profession, was much in demand for stage engagements, resulting in her having to spend most of her time in America. The Major was given a new job, which required that he visit the outposts of the Empire, to check that the army was in good heart. As a result their paths seldom crossed. Absence in their case did not make the heart grow fonder. Frustration convinced them the marriage was not working. They agreed, quite amicably, to divorce. It was expedient that the lady provide the evidence, which she willingly did.

Because of his many absences abroad, the Major reckoned it desirable his mail be redirected to his lawyer, who had instructions to open, and if necessary attend to anything of a business nature, and to retain unopened anything which appeared personal.

Came the day when a cable arrived from U.S.A. The lawyer felt duty bound to open. The message read – "Darling, are we divorced? Love. Vera."

THE FIRE (2)

"You ask me, Duncan, 'What the blazes is going on?'

To answer your question, I've been to the site of the fire, so that I know a little about it.

"I have seen the two surfacemen who maintain the line adjoining Drumcraig. They were quite willing to speak to me, but wouldn't sign statements. That is reasonable, and is enough meantime."

"What had they to say."

"In dry weather, south bound trains nearly always discharge sparks which set vegetation alight. For the most part they cause no danger. When the fires look dangerous they beat them out. In this case they could not establish control. I have their names and addresses, and told them I would not disclose to their employees what they told me."

"Where does that take us?"

"A bit along the road, but we have a long way to go. I found a retired engine driver who gave me a statement to the effect that fire boxes of engines on that line, are not fitted with spark arresters – because they give rise to a reduction in power. When the engines are labouring up a steep hill they are prone to cause a discharge of sparks.

"I have also written to the Railway area manager, asking permission to interview staff. Unfortunately he cannot deal with this. He has referred to his legal department which is a pity."

"Why?"

"Because I think I know the legal adviser, and expect no co–operation from him. He is a tough and unreasonable cookie."

"Can't we force them to give evidence?"

"Maybe, but let's leave that for the moment.

"The Fire Brigade are prepared to help, and of course the estate workers."

"What I want to know is when can we start a fire in the court against the bloody railway? They're burning up moors and forests all over the place, and nobody does a blind thing to stop them."

"Are you quite determined to take action?"

"Yes."

"Well, I have to warn you it will be a very expensive business, and if you lose, you will be down thousands of pounds."

"But you're my legal adviser. You should know if I have a case. Seems obvious to me."

"Think about this. The fire did not come directly to you from the railway line. The fire spread to you from Drumcraig. Maybe you would have to go for Drumcraig and not the railway company."

"Good God. That would be useless. He's as poor as a church mouse. He's a member of Lloyds, and his syndicate is up to the neck in claims for the American earthquake. He must be about broke."

"I've had a look into the law on the subject. You can claim on the Railway Company and be paid automatically without proof of fault. Such a claim would be restricted to £200."

"That's just stupid. Forget it."

"O.K. Otherwise you have to prove negligence. It is my view you can make it stick on the railway company. But this is a pretty big case, and I want my view confirmed. Do you agree I should get opinion of Counsel?"

"Certainly, if that's what you want to do."

"O.K. I'll attend to that, and we can discuss it again when we have opinion. Meantime, while the present dry weather continues I want a watch kept on the line for at least two weeks to record and plot on a map all fires started by engines between 7 a.m. and 5 p.m. Can you get someone to do that?"

"Yes. I have a young trainee factor in the office. That would be something useful for him to do for a change."

"Then we have to quantify your claim. We need an experienced surveyor to do that."
"Are you recommending anyone?"
"Yes. I have worked before with Ian Rose of Stirling. He's a seventy year old, but pretty fit. He has a first class brain."
"All right. Get him."
"I already have, by phone. I'll arrange for him to inspect as soon as possible. I've also intimated a claim against the Railway Company for an unspecified amount. It will be rejected."

ROY THE DOG

Roy was a three year old collie dog of the most amiable disposition. He was a great friend of all the children in the street. He saw them off to school, and he welcomed them back to play with him.

Roy had one aversion – sticks. When Antonia (a bad natured little shrew anyway) made her way home carrying a hockey stick, he stood his distance. Whether Antonia wanted to make up to the dog or to cause bodily harm was not clear. Roy took the latter view, and gave warning by nipping her ankle, without breaking the skin.

Antonia went howling home to Mum Antonia, who was the mother of a shrew, and who raised hell. The Police were brought in. Such pressure was brought to bear that the Chief Constable brought proceedings in the Burgh Police Court.

Mr partner, Robert, was asked to appear and plead "Not Guilty." The case went to trial. Robert was unworried – after all a dog is entitled to one bite, and up till now Roy had an unblemished character. At the trial Baillie Davidson found the case proved and ordered the dog to be destroyed.

Consternation on the part of Robert, Roy's mum, and all the neighbours who knew and loved Roy for his good nature and playful ways.

Robert was consulted on the question of appeal. In no uncertain terms he advised an appeal was bound to succeed. But what about expense? The neighbours met and set up a fund for Roy's appeal. Twenty four of them contributed.

The case went to Edinburgh and Baillie Davidson's decision was overturned. Great joy in the street, and Robert was the hero. "The dog's advocate" they called him.

When he next went to the Sheriff Court, the Faculty Wag congratulated Robert on his triumph, and enquired – "Since you did your stuff so well for a dog, would you do the same for a bitch?"

CASTING BREAD ON WATER.
A CLIENT OF MEANS.

I had a senior who used to quote – "Cast thy bread upon the waters."

Immediately after World War II there was a burst of entrepreneurial activity. Companies were being formed almost monthly, and small businesses established.

Two bright lads came along to have a partnership agreement prepared. Motor vehicles were unobtainable, and their choice was bicycles. They gathered together a group of boy cyclists, who, after school hours, delivered goods to whomsoever was willing to hire them. And there was lots of custom. But returns were small, and the boys were erratic.

After a year the bright lads came to say they wanted to put a van or vans on the road to do the same work, and to include deliveries for local shopkeepers. The pre–war "bowsher" had faded from the picture.

This brought us into the sphere of Road Traffic Licensing, about which I knew nothing, and admitted it. I asked for time.

I read about A, B, and C licences, and the attitude of the Transport Commissioner to applications for new licences. 'A' licences could be written off. They were for long distance work. Any applicant was hammered before the Traffic Court by British Road Services and British Rail. It was regarded as a closed shop. 'B' licences were granted for short distance work, and the goods carried, restricted. Likewise, applications for 'B's' faced massive opposition from existing operators. 'C' licences were for owners of vehicles carrying their own goods, and were granted automatically.

So my interest had to be for a 'B' licence.

My investigations revealed that one good excuse for the grant of a 'B' licence was that the applicant would put a horse off the road. I advised the aspirants to get a horse and cart, use it for a year, and for this no licence was required. This was done. Theirs was the only horse regularly negotiating the narrow streets of the town centre, to the consternation of other road users, and the Police. But it was within the law, and those who didn't like it couldn't do a blind thing about it.

When the year was up, application for a B licence was heard in the Burgh Police Courthouse in Castle Wynd. There was substantial opposition from other hauliers, notably MacBraynes, who were also well organised for court hearings. A restricted licence was granted, thanks very largely to the evidence of the Provost of Inverness, Mr Hugh Ross, who had a licensed grocer's business in Queensgate. The Commissioner, Mr. Robertson was quite impressed that his court should be graced by the presence of the Provost whom he was meeting for the first time.

For me that was the start of Road Licensing court work, little favoured by my legal colleagues because it was new to them. Work flowed in. Among those who came my way was John Macleod, who had two lorries running from Rhiconich in North West Sutherland near Kinlochbervie. Around 1951 Mr. Macleod's business was purchased by the Trustees of the Duke of Westminster, who continued also with Macleod's lawyer.

The Agent for the Trustees, whom I was to come to know so well was Col. Robert Neilson, but he did not employ me blind. Before our first meeting he satisfied himself I had some knowledge of Traffic Courts. He had one question for me to answer.

"Are you a Mason?"

"God," I thought. "If he wants me to join the masons before signing me on, I've had it. Because I won't."

I gave my answer firmly – "No."

"Right, you're on. I don't want any bloody masons in the family."

I was chuffed.

There followed much Road Licensing work, buses as well as Haulage, because the Trustees also owned Sutherland Transport Co., Lairg, who ran passenger vehicles.

Robert was ambitious. He wanted an A licence. That was a battle. The big guns of British Rail, British Road Services, and MacBraynes were out in force. The hearing occupied one and a half days. We had a good case to argue – the rapidly developing fishing port of Kinlochbervie, the communications required to the Trustees main base at Chester, the need to have access to the English ports with fish, and return loads to make the journeys viable, the employment being created by the Trustees in a remote Highland area.

The outcome was that an A licence was granted for two vehicles.

Robert was in high glee. He shepherded his team, lawyer and witnesses, to the Station Hotel and ordered champagne. I can still see his glowing boyish face as he raised his glass – "I'm sure His Grace would wish us to celebrate this auspicious occasion."

More work flowed – the formation of Pulford (Scotland) Ltd. to run the transport and sea fishing business at Kinlochbervie, where an ice plant and a deep freeze store were established. A company was also formed to run a small boatyard, where minor repairs could be affected to the fishing boats. Premises were purchased at Aberdeen harbour, to facilitate the handling of Kinlochbervie fish without the intervention of a middleman, and to secure traffic by road to southern markets. Besides the haulage, forestry, sea fishing, and boatyard businesses, there was a substantial interest in agriculture – over a thousand breeding ewes, about a hundred Galloways. Morangie farm in Tain was purchased to complement the hill farming activity at Reay, the North West Sutherland estate – 480 acres arable and 200 rough. Add the sporting – stalking, perhaps the best sea trout fishing in Scotland, superb salmon fishing.

Money was being pumped into the North West Sutherland area without thought of return. It was a joy to be associated with a laird who had the good of the area at heart to the extent of providing work for 275 employees on and around Reay Forest Estate.

There was always something interesting going on.

The Trustees wanted to plant trees under a Dedication Scheme, to take advantage of Government grants. Their Forestry Adviser reckoned the land was suitable, but the Forestry Commission would not sanction Dedication, because of the quality of the land. It was agreed in a negotiation with the Commission that the estate go ahead, and if, after ten years, the estate had proved its point, the land would be accepted for Dedication.

A fishery expert was employed to advise on fish stocks in Loch Stack being adversely affected by sub standard fish entering the loch via the Laxford river. The only method of control was to build a fish trap across the river – a cruive, as it is called in Scotland. Both banks of the river were owned by the Trustees. Robert was at this time a member of the Advisory Panel, which preceded the formation of the Highland Board, and had access to civil servants in Edinburgh. They told him such a project was illegal. True or false? I did not know. What I did know was that all the fishing rights vested formerly in the Duke of Sutherland had been conveyed to the trustees. I would have to see the Duke's Title. Could I order an extract from the Land Register? Yes, of course. When it came through it proved to be in manuscript, about sixty pages, in Latin. I had to ask my friend David Thom, the Classics Master at Inverness Academy for a translation. He was fascinated to handle Scottish Legal Latin, which he had never met before. He pinpointed the one expression I wanted – "cum piscionibus," – in English – "with fishings." Expressed in this form, it meant fishings of all kinds. I told Robert I

11

disagreed with his friends in Edinburgh, and suggested he go ahead and see what happened. He did, and nothing happened.

Robert had appointed Colin Campbell as an assistant. Colin had trained as a pilot in the Fleet Air Arm. This gave rise to a suggestion a plane should be purchased to minimise travel time between the North West, Inverness, Aberdeen, and Chester. So the pair of them ran a three seater for a year, when Headquarters ruled the cost was outrageous, and the plane sold. But not before I had a few jaunts in it myself.

I had a friend Alex Mackenzie, a Tobacconist, but with a passion for boats. He started experimenting with glass fibre on a wooden mould for the construction of loch fishing boats, and was very successful, but not in convincing the public that a glass boat was safe. I had sailed with the fishing fleets in Mallaig and Fraserburgh, and noticed that when the boats went to sea, they had a clutter of wooden fish boxes on deck, lashed down. The life span of a wooden box was about five road journeys. I suggested to Robert Neilson, that if glass fibre boxes were used, constructed to nest, the clutter on the boat decks would be avoided, and the boxes would have a much longer life span. He readily agreed, and after seeing samples, ordered a hundred. The fishermen liked them, but there was serious opposition from vested interests, the timber box trade, and many of them mysteriously disappeared. So, initially, they were unsuccessful. Now, they are universal.

A final story. When His Grace the Duke died, a service was arranged to be held in the village hall at Achfarry. Robert instructed that I attend, and I sat beside a young English man, Maurice Taylor, who was then the manager of Sutherland Transport Company.

The lament was to be played by Seton Gordon. He was a well known piper as well as a distinguished naturalist. When the moment came, Seton retired to the side room to start his pipe, but the lungs had lost their youthful ardour. He was quite an old man by now and he had the greatest difficulty getting the drones to function. He walked slowly into the hall – and still no drones, and puff, and puff. I was really sorry for the man, to the extent of personal embarrassment. In the midst of all this Maurice whispered to me – "What's the name of the tune, Dick?"

Looking back on that era – bread on waters, for thou shalt find it after many days.

CHAMBER OF COMMERCE – AIRBORNE.

I was youngish, and Secretary of the Chamber of Commerce.

Captain E.E. Fresson was dismissed as an employee of British Airways, to the rancour of many who admired his pioneering qualities, and had utilised his air services to the islands of the north.

The Chamber decided to hold a public protest meeting, and discussed who should be the speakers from the platform. Eric Linklater was an obvious choice. He was an outspoken admirer of Fresson. Jack Macleod, Liberal National M.P. for Ross and Cromarty, was another obvious choice – a good speaker who would make his points without hogging it. The M.P. for Inverness–shire was Sir Murdoch Macdonald, by then up in years. He started off as a Liberal, but became a Liberal national like Jack

Macleod. He had to be invited, as a matter of courtesy, but the other two were invited first, with a view to putting Sir Murdoch on last because he never knew when to stop, and he was wont to waffle.

Before I got around to sending Sir Murdoch his invitation, he came storming into my office. What did I mean by inviting an M.P. for an adjoining constituency into his without first consulting him? Was I not aware of the insult that was? It was quite unpardonable. He was going to see Major Ross, my senior employer, and also Dr. Evan Barron, Editor of the Inverness Courier to have me denounced. His rage was ungovernable, close to apoplectic. I offered no defence, except that I had instructions to invite him too. That was no excuse. Macleod was invited first. There was little more I could say. Anything I said might have been quoted as the view of the Chamber of Commerce. So I took it on the chin.

I was on quite good terms with Major Ross, although I had some brushes with him, sometimes enough to receive the edge of his tongue. I did not know what was his relationship with Sir Murdoch, but as they were contemporaries, I reckoned it would be quite warm. I dared not think how Major Ross would tear me to shreds. If he thought as Sir Murdoch thought, I expected to be on the look out for another job.

After a sufficient pause to allow Sir Murdoch air his views to the major, I was summoned into the presence.

This was it.

"What have you been doing to Sir Murdoch Dick?"

As calmly as I could, I told him the story. He listened patiently.

"Och you don't need to worry about Sir Murdoch. He's a stupid old bugger anyway." What of the meeting? It was a great success. The Town Hall was crowded. And the result? Nothing.

ROUGH JUSTICE

Back before the war, John MacBean was a young, up and coming, ambitious young lawyer, with a penchant for court work.

For a client, John had pleaded "Not Guilty" to a charge of violence, and the case went to trial.

At that time, the Prosecutor in the Police Court was the Chief Constable, MacNaughton, a staunch and firm upholder of the law within the Burgh. John was determined top put up a good fight for his client, and had prepared carefully for the contest with the Prosecutor. He also had a number of cases to cite favourable to his cause, and these were contained in hefty leather bound tomes.

John entered the court in the Castle Wynd with two of these under each arm.

The courtroom was small and shabby. The public benches were ranged in high steps behind the solicitors' table, and were crowded. The court was a resort of many long term unemployed. It was a warm place to be in, and it offered a dose of entertainment, for good measure. Presided over by a Baillie without knowledge of the law, it was a source of rough justice for the delinquent citizens of Inverness.

At the sight of John and his books, the Chief's jaw dropped, and he blurted out angrily –

"We don't want any of your bloody law here."

Hamish was a prominent businessman and gentleman farmer. For him attendance at the Agricultural Show in the Bught Park was a must. He was making his way home after a happy day, in his brand new Wolsey, driving cautiously, because the roadway was cluttered with pedestrians. Early on a bright summer evening, the sun was shining. A young Policeman, wearing puttees which indicated the County force, imported to help with the traffic problem caused by the show, stopped Hamish to tell him his headlights were burning – purely a matter of courtesy. As Hamish rolled down his side window to take the message, the Policeman visibly winced when assaulted by a powerful blast of the best Queen Mary's Seal.

That was why Hamish found himself in the Burgh Police Office, whence I was called by the duty Sergeant, two hours later.

Hamish had been through the usual humiliating drill – pockets emptied and deprived of braces and tie, lodged in a cell with a concrete floor, horse hair paliasse, and toilet flushed by remote control. The heavy metal door equipped with a peep–hole and a massive lock.

The Police Doctor had attended, and noted Hamish could not walk along a chalk line, stand on one leg, or conduct a coherent conversation. The breath smelt, and the eyes betrayed. Breathalyser? It hadn't been heard of. Pathologist for blood and urine tests? There was no pathologist.

Hamish had been formally charged – drunk in charge of a car. From that point he was the property of the Fiscal who served the Sheriff Court.

I offered comfort and said I would try to have him released.

In my phone call to the Fiscal, I reported no damage to person or property; no other vehicle involved; no complaint by a member of the public; no resistance to the Police; complete co–operation with the Police Doctor; a well known citizen with business and residence in town. I undertook to secure his appearance in court the next day. With his usual show of reluctance the Fiscal agreed Hamish be released, and so instructed the duty Sergeant, who was delighted to be relieved of the responsibility of holding a prisoner.

In the Charge Room Hamish's belongings were returned. He could not find his pockets to replace his wallet, loose change, keys or cigarettes.

He had no hope of replacing his tie, or braces unaided.

In the midst of all the fumbling, and sotto voce mumbling, he turned to me with big innocent bloodshot eyes and enquired – "You don't think I'm drunk, do you Dick?"

He found a way of doing without his car for a year.

14

THE FIRE (3)

In time Opinion of Counsel arrived and I sent it to Duncan, which caused him to call again.

"That looks all right," he said. "Where do we go now?"

"Still determined to sue?"

"Don't ask such damn silly questions. Can we get on with it?"

"I warn you again, taking a case to the Court of Session is a very expensive business, especially if you lose. The Railway Company will take you to the cleaners."

"But if you say, and Counsel says I have a good case, how can I lose?"

"No–one can predict the outcome of a court case. Apart from the expense there is the question of time. It will take two to three years to get a final verdict. You'll probably pester the life out of me over that period. In case we fall out, as we have done in the past, you might as well be thinking of someone to take over from me."

"Bloody law. Anyway, get cracking."

"I can't get cracking till I know how much we are suing for."

"Can't you just stick in a figure – say £20,000?"

"No. Each item in your claim must be spoken to. In any case we shall have a figure from Rose within two days. You will see it to be much more than you had in mind. That's why I recommended Rose. I've also asked Archie Finlay to support Rose, and he will."

Archie was one of the most prominent sheep farmers in Sutherland.

"Did you get statements from the Fire Brigade people?"

"Yes. I also wrote adjoining proprietors asking if they would join with you in attacking the railway. Two said "No." Three did not reply. One said "Yes," and he is Mackenzie in West Farm. He was least affected, so he couldn't be expected to contribute much to costs as he is farming in such a small way.

I've also heard from the Legal Adviser to the Railway Company. He will not discuss your claim, and will not give access to staff, or the engine sheds for inspection of the engines."

"What next?"

"We can ask the court for access, but only if an action has been commenced. I suggest we ask Counsel to serve, and then apply for the access we require."

"all right. Carry on."

"One other thing. We need expert rail engineers to examine all the engines, if and when we get access. The only experts in the country are rail employees, so we have to go to the continent. Through the Chamber of Commerce I have been given the names of two Belgians, English speakers, who are highly recommended. I want your consent to employ them."

"Suppose you must."

The Edinburgh correspondents were instructed to have the action commenced for the figure brought out by Rose, and using skeleton pleadings, and to make immediate application for access to the engines, B.R. Staff, and records.

SHERIFF COURT CAMEOS

A visitor to the Castle Wynd in Inverness on a Thursday morning about ten, would be forgiven for thinking a meeting of the Presbytery was about to take place. He would see a trail of soberly dressed gentlemen meandering up the brae, each carrying a little black book. No, it was not a kirk occasion. It comprised members of the Faculty heading for the Sheriff Court, where pleas were heard in civil cases. The black books were court diaries, in which the solicitors had entered the cases entrusted to them, and on which they would be required to speak. I often wondered why the lawyers adopted such solemn demeanours. They looked as though they bore the cares of the world.

The Faculty congregated in the Faculty Hall, a very large dignified room, a huge table running down the centre, and walls lined by glass fronted book cases, crammed with books. In the far corner of the room was a door leading to a wee room which contained the most beautiful piece of blue and white Victorian china ever to serve a twentieth century purpose. A swing on the hanging chain brought down a cascade of water like Rogie Falls in spate. I wonder what supplementary diversion this caused after the invasion of the Faculty by the fair sex. The court room was quite a distinguished apartment, withe elevated bench at one end, fronted by the well, with provision for clerk, prosecutor, jury, solicitors, newsmen and a witness stand. The public ranged behind, and above in a gallery at the back.

The roof was so high that every utterance was lost in the clouds, and there were constant complaints that the lawyers mumbled.

All except Murdo McIntosh, the Sheriff Clerk.

Loud mouthed Murdo ruled his court with little deference to the Sheriff, like an evangelical preacher in full flight. He loved Latin tags, and delighted in announcing the Sheriff "ex proprio motu," or the fiscal deserted "pro loco et tempore," or in a claim for compensation there was no "consursus debiti et crediti."

Allow me to tell one of the many stories Murdo inspired. I was not present when this occurred but it was given to me on very good authority, and with ample corroboration.

In Small Debt cases, if to be defended, the nature of the defence had to be stated orally at the bar. In one such case one of my colleagues defending, stated the sum sued for was not due. Murdo had a look at the statement of account attached to the summons, and found entered a number of payments to account. These constituted an admission of debt, if not of amount. Murdo bawled out – "Your defence is no bloody good, but,"

and he cocked a thumb over his shoulder to the bench – "We'll see what this b.... thinks of it."

Sheriff Grant was a patient man. In civil cases he was very seldom overturned, but his judgements were painfully slow in appearing. He was lithe, invariably garbed in a kilt, which he carried to perfection. Visiting solicitors were amused when he stopped proceedings to fish into his stocking for his Skean Dhu to sharpen his pencil.

Despite the occasional excesses of Murdo McIntosh, the Sheriff presided over a tight court, which dispensed justice, in accord with the highest traditions of the profession.

The Sheriff sat bare headed. He wore no gown, nor did the solicitors or court officials. But the Lord Advocate decided to rule, for the preservation of the dignity of the court, that the Sheriff be attired in wig and gown, and other participants in gowns.

I continued in court work after the change, and could not see that it made one whit of difference to the efficacy of the court. Let pageantry evoke wonder, not fear. Here's a case where I would revert to the older ways. In my estimation the use of "Court rig" by the profession tends to intimidate, and to widen the gap between the profession and the public. It is a badge of office, like that of a Traffic Warden – power with pomposity. It contributes to the vanity of the solicitor, in providing an ego boost. What more gratifying to self esteem than a prance through the Castle corridors, gown flowing Dracula style. It is theatre, pantomime, stupid, unnecessary. Hallowe'en every day. The gown is a discomfort to the wearer, practical only as a dust jacket. It complicates the kit of a lawyer travelling to "away" courts, it is a clutter in the cloakroom, and a nuisance to identify among uniform garments.

At the same time perhaps we could rid ourselves of the now vulgar designation of "solicitor". It is granted of authentically ancient origin, but the meaning has been debased to quite an inelegant connotation. "Lawyer" is much better, and undeniably descriptive. I can hear the ladies at the bar approve – and they are rapidly nearing parity in numbers. Perhaps one day soon we shall be hearing "the law is a lass."

One of the Sheriff's great loves was the Highland Bagpipe. He was both exponent and judge.

At a sitting of the Criminal Court there was a string of cases involving speeding. As each was called, a solicitor bobbed up and pleaded "guilty,"

followed by a plea in mitigation, sometimes brief, often far too long. Frequently John commenced – "This is a most unusual case, my lord." The Sheriff kept most meticulous notes, and frequently entered – "Def. J.McB. MUC."

Irrespective of mitigating circumstances, the Sheriff handed all the standard fine at the time of £2. Throughout the platitudinous pleas, Athole, a quiet man and a piper, sat silently, a pencil in his hands held like a chanter. He was absently fingering "Barren Rocks of Aden."

When his case called he rose –

"Guilty, my lord. Nothing to say."

"Fine £1."

AT SEA

Robert had a client at Glenelg, who had a farming interest – sheep. Requiring additional grazing he took a lease of the island Pabay lying less than a mile off Broadford. Using local boats the sheep movements became uneconomic, so the client decided to run his own boat. A rather ancient thirty foot, ex Admiralty harbour launch with a Kelvin petrol/paraffin engine was purchased and entrusted to the Thornbush Slipway to make sea worthy. She was called Proserpine – Queen of the Infernal Regions, wife of Pluto, Ruler of Hell.

To get the boat to Glenelg meant hiring a crew of three for at least a week – expensive.

Robert, who was quite a boyish man with a lot of spunk, asked me if I would join with him in ferrying the Proserpine to Glenelg. Agreed, and the crew comprised we two, Hugh Macleod an engineer, and Douglas David, an insurance manager, ex driver of an army tank.

First, to test the boat in the Firth, we bought in some petrol and paraffin, and set off on a summer evening. After much coughing and spluttering, we sailed as far as Chanonry Point. More the engine refused. We hailed a local speed launch and were towed ignominiously back to harbour. We didn't know that lamp paraffin which we bought, was not the stuff for a Kelvin.

Under pressure of parents, we were induced to take with us also two fifteen year olds – Jimmy South and Alan Hill. This was against my better judgement, as there were risks attached to the passage we proposed. However the parents accepted the risk on behalf of their offspring, so they were included.

Of an evening, we took the boat round from the harbour to the Canal.

I got rows from some of the Keepers for entering the locks too fast, though at the slowest speed of the engine. I found the idea was – kick ahead, and stop, kick ahead, and stop. Later, I found that half the engine block could be shut off, to allow us drive on two only of the four cylinders – a help.

We were equipped with compass (from the Sea Cadets) and charts. We anchored at south Bona, where Willie Macdonald, ex lighthouse keeper at North Bona, took us ashore.

Next morning, a Thursday, we raised anchor early to go through the Canal to Corpach. On the reach to the top lock at Corpach, we encountered a huge Dutch cargo vessel, and I aimed, as I should, to pass port to port. But she did not return the compliment, and at the last seconds I gave two toots on the klaxon, hauled round to port, only to see the bottom coming up to meet me. Like driving a bike, I corrected the helm and slid down the starboard side of the Dutchman with inches to spare.

We were sorry to learn at the locks, the Dutchman went aground, having lost steerage in such confined waters, and had to be winched off.

Digs for the night had been arranged at Fort William.

Sailing had to be delayed on Friday to take advantage of the tide through Corran narrows. We arrived early evening at Oban, where again digs had been arranged.

Robert was acting as quartermaster and cook, and wore a sailor's blue jean which I had dug up for him. He handled the primus stove expertly, and produced tea, bangers, bacon, chops, fried bread, and potatoes, to the entire satisfaction of the crew. Otherwise sustenance came from tins and bottles. But I made it an absolute rule, no alcohol was to be consumed while at sea, and I threatened to quit if I was disobeyed. I was not.

On Saturday the fair weather we had enjoyed so far, deserted us. The rain tippled down. We left Oban in the afternoon, at a time suitable for the tide through the Sound of Mull, and arrived at Tobermory, where no digs were booked. At 6 p.m. the harbour was crowded – not a bit of harbour wall to be seen where we could moor. We were soaked, tired, and hungry. In desperation, we came alongside a MacBrayne boat and hailed the bridge, from which the skipper appeared.

"Can we stay alongside till the morning, please?"

"Och aye. We won't be going out tomorrow."

Of course not. Tomorrow was Sunday.

Then into the town to look for lodgings for the night. The place was choc–a–block with summer visitors. Another six could in no way be accommodated. We reached the stage of considering sleeping rough on the front, when a lady answered our knock on the door, of a most unprepossessing tall house. She responded to our hard luck story. She had taken entry to the house only a day or two before, and was redecorating with a view to entering the bed and breakfast competition. She had empty rooms, absolutely empty, and we were welcome to sleep on the floor. She could supply a hot meal,and dry off our clothes. Done, – we ate, and we slept, and we were up early in the morning. Our saviour was well recompensed.

Down at the boat we saw fog, not dense, but certainly fog. Depressing. MacBrayne's skipper told us the forecast was that it would lift in course of the forenoon. A decision was required – for or against? Unanimous – for. Out we went, setting a course of 290 degrees to clear Ardnamurchan Point.

Our luck was out. The fog thickened, visibility fifty yards. The next decision was mine. Go on, or go back? Better to be in fog in open seas than in confined waters. Go on.

But for safety the route had to be altered. The intention was to pass by Ardnamurchan Point. But it couldn't be seen, and the fog horn was waiting. So, continue on 290 degrees for an extra half hour before turning north to 030 degrees, and dead reckoning through the Sound of Sleat, with nothing to be seen. I was nervous. Then came a ripple on the water from the south west, and the curtain rose a little to reveal what I had earnestly hoped to see – Isle Oronsay Light. Great. I could follow up the Skye coast, which I did in complete contentment – till I suddenly found myself in a fast flowing river, doubling the speed. Hard round to starboard, for this could be the tidal race at Kylerhea. Out of the race, we could follow the mainland to the east, round to Glenelg. Dwellings straggle along the coastline at Glenelg, and the roadway beyond them could be seen but not a soul in sight. Why should the populous be indoors on such a good afternoon? It was the Sabbath. I put my binoculars on the houses for a better look. Almost all had a window open with a telescope poking through.

We were not long tied up alone at the jetty, when the local bobby appeared, to check we carried no contraband. He was a cheery soul, but he would not have a dram. When we pointed out he could come on board and be shielded from view by the engine canopy, that was different.

Robert's client owned the local pub. Attached to it was a shed which was to be our abode for the night. Donald, the shepherd, had instructions to prepare it for us. He had not done so. Clearly our bedroom was the abode of the local hen population, for the whole of its area was covered with droppings. The only furniture was two single spring beds, in a shocking state. Robert phoned Donald to appear immediately. When he did he was subjected to the most almighty drubbing he ever experienced on a Sabbath. "Get brushes, get blankets, get pillows, and something to serve as groundsheets – and where are we going to wash? In the sink in the pub.

I can still picture Jimmy, a towel over his shoulder, going gaily for his badly needed wash, and turning the tap, only to find it was beer that flowed. The joy of innocence.

I have often seen pubs with floors of sawdust. Never, till now, did I meet one with floor of henshit.

After a restless night, we were collected by our chummy taximan from Inverness next day.

Three years later the lease of Pabay expired, and was not renewed. We took

19

Proserpine through Crinan to the Clyde for disposal. But we were hardened mariners by then, and Donald, the Shepherd, showed he had benefited from his earlier experience. He provided very comfortable rooms in his own house. There was one snag – Robert could not get sleep for the drip, the constant drip in a cistern in the roof space. Sometimes it was matched to a grandfather clock, with a steady beat – tick tock, or drip drop. That would have been bearable, but for the fact the timing would change without warning, to that of a spring wind alarm clock – a fast tick, tick, tick, or drip, drip, drip. There was a third movement like the alarm going off – slush, slush, whizz. He was vexed, Robert, but contrasting it with the previous henhouse abode, it was heaven. So he kept his peace. He even chatted up Donald, keeping an equable temper.

"How many children now, Donald?"

"Four."

"What? Four in four years? How many more will you have?"

"No more. Four's enough. Definitely no more."

"Well you'd better get that loft cistern fixed up quick."

MOCK TRIAL

The Boy Scouts were short of funds. They came to me with the request that I stage a mock trial. I hadn't thought of it. But it seemed possible, though I never fancied myself as an impresario.

First thing was to decide on the charge – nothing too heavy like murder, or even violence. Poaching, that was the best idea. Could give rise to a few laughs. And it would have to be ad lib. Even if I wrote out the whole script, the people I had in mind would not stick to it. SO I wrote a skeleton simply to give the players an idea of how to proceed.

First, the lawyers.

Gordon Munro, I thought, had a good face for a judge, and Robert Forrest and Ian Witherspoon could prosecute and defend. We had a natural comedian in Rory Mackay, who would do for the poacher. He was a great Ness–speak. Willie Michie the local auctioneer, purveyor of wit if not wisdom, was so funny that the women of the town turned out to listen to his patter on the rostrum, without any intention to buy.

Nobody could compete with George Proctor, our Sheriff Clerk, for the part of Clerk of Court.

The very successful local concert party, the Florians, threw in one or two witnesses, and George MacBean of their number, and the Burgh Registrar, would do the make up. Harry Leishman, Manager of General Accident, and member of the Scout Executive Committee was happy to play Minister of Religion, and a couple of my own staff, Policemen.

At the early planning stage, it all looked too easy. All those I approached gladly agreed to co–operate.

Then I met a snag. One or two senior members of the Faculty, who had been left out of my plans, put their heads together, and came up with the view that I was bringing the profession into disrepute. No way should we go ahead without the say so of the Faculty in general meeting, and of the Sheriff. I gave a bit of thought to the complaint, and concluded that it was nit picking. I perceived that the objectors had attempted to act as censors, and did not find such interference acceptable. The lawyer boys on my team agreed, so we ignored the opposition.

The Northern Meeting readily agreed to let is have free use of their Supper Room, in the ground floor of their rooms in Church Street.

Tickets were printed, and the trial advertised.

Next, I thought necessary to hold a couple of trial runs. Could I get the damned lawyers to agree to a date? Twice, three times, I put pressure on by telephone, but no date. In despair I called together the other members of the cast and covered the ground with them. The Florians, perfectionists, were mightily displeased I could not arrange a full briefing. The whole business was getting so desperate, I feared the lawyers would pull out. And this is a bitchy one from me – I was glad the lawyers were not intended to be star quality, but any lawyer who does not prepare his brief does not deserve success. Their function was to present the openings for the witnesses to deploy their wit and wisdom. To help nail them, I gave a hand out to the press, naming the cast. If they were known publicly as participants, it might not be so easy for them to renegue. Their view was "We shall act as we do in Court, and require no drilling – and positively not from you."

Time went by and still no rehearsals.

The day came to put on the show, which never deserved to succeed. The date chosen was 28th February 1955. It snowed in the morning, the afternoon, and the evening. By 7 p.m. six inches of the stuff lay picturesquely on the streets of Inverness. And all the tickets were sold. The crowds rolled in, all on foot. Motoring was impossible. Not only that, but a ticketless drove gathered at the door, begging admission – standing room, at any price. But we showed no avarice. A limited number were allowed to stand at half price. It was to my deep embarrassment I had to refuse access to several close personal friends, simply because there was no corner in which they could be accommodated.

I've never been in such a state of jitters. The thought crossed my mind – why shouldn't I run away?

Too late. The Court was assembling. The Clerk called for order, and the charge read – poaching for rabbits. Rory Mackay pled "Not Guilty," and assured the Sheriff he didn't like rabbits anyway.

That set the tone. The lawyers didn't matter much, but they did their stuff to move the action on.

The Policemen told of the arrest, and Willie Michie, magnificently attired in ladies' clothes, as the local busy body, delighted by the limelight, confirmed she saw Rory come from the wood with a bag in his hand.

Alan Cameron of the Florians, as the Keeper, with a great grudge against Rory, said he had often seen Rory in the wood and knew he had a gun.

The two lover birds from the Florians had been doing a bit of snogging in the wood. The lady dressed as a 1920 flapper with knee length skirt, cloche hat, and a string of pearls hanging down to her knees. This she gathered in one hand and persisted in

21

swinging it in circles while giving evidence. She was a howl. She had heard gunfire and feared for some shot in her bum. Her boy friend gallantly gave protection by lying on top of her, which he much enjoyed.

Jim Harper, the butcher, and another two Florians gave Rory what amounted to an alibi. Harry Leishman, as the Minister spoke to Rory's character, so much better that the average Minister could, but clearly as a stranger to the truth.

The summing up did not matter much. As arranged the finding was "Not Guilty," and the audience gave a roar of approval.

I couldn't believe it. The smiling faces walking out into the winter night said it all.

Never would I do such a thing again.

Back row – Jim Harper, Butcher, for the accused; Bob Mactaggart , Accountant and Gilbert Thomson, Clerk, both of South Forrest and MacKintosh, and ??? witnesses for the prosecution.

Middle row – Rory Mackay, Solicitor; Innes and Mackay the accused poachers; Robert Forrest of South Forrest representing the Crown; Gordon Munro of Munro and Noble; Ian Wotherspoon of Macandrew and Jenkins, defending; Sheriff; George Proctor, Sheriff Clerk and acting as such here; Harry Leishman, Manager, General Accident, character witness for the accused and representing the cloth; two ladies ??

Front row – Willie Michie, Auctioneer witness for prosecution; Alan Cameron of Inverness Gas Works, Keeper for prosecution.

LIQUOR.

Liquor licensing could not be avoided.

The court granted new licences almost under protest. To appear for a new applicant was to face massive barriers. Firstly, the court, all laymen, Magistrates and J.P.'s, required to approve. Their discretion was absolute and their reluctance proverbial, whatever the evidence. Then came the objectors, the Temperance Movement, the Church, the Licensed Trade (strange bedfellows) and neighbouring proprietors and residents. Finally, the Police. Every new licence increased their supervisory obligations. They detested any increase in licensed outlets.

The applicant entered the court handicapped. A case which, in a court of law, would be considered proved, did not necessarily succeed in the liquor court because of the absolute discretion vested in the members. So often it looked as though a closed shop policy was in operation. Existing licensees were also at risk. They were required to apply for renewal each year. Objections might be raised to renewal by practically anybody, and especially the Police, and by members of the court, without notice.

The Police frowned upon a licencee who for any reason refused to supply a meal, whenever requested. If they had a complaint, they similarly put at risk the licence of one who closed down over the winter months. This was particularly hard on small country hotels who depended solely on summer trade for their continued existence. It mattered little if the public were adequately served by adjoining hotels in the area. The whole set up was stupid in the extreme.

All was changed by the explosion in the tourist industry in the sixties and seventies. If the applicant was suitable, and the premises suitable, you were in. The tourist must be served. The tourist rules – O.K.? The easement of law restricting hours of sale was an earnest of change in the public perceptions of licensing.

Gilbert had a small hotel with a pub, and a six day licence. Across the road, his competitor, Tom, was in the same position. Gilbert was to have an autumn break, a holiday abroad. He had reason to believe Tom had designs on a seven day licence. I was to watch the advertisement of applications, and if need arose, oppose an extension to the opposite side of the street. There is an obligation on the Clerk of Court to advertise applications in two newspapers circulating locally. The local papers, were the Courier, Highland News, Herald, and Chronicle. The Herald had a very restricted circulation, and the Chronicle was directed to farmers. So the Courier and the Highland News carried the adverts., and these did not include the one I was looking for. But I happened to be in court on other business, and I heard called the very application I was charged to oppose.

Indignantly, I rose and told the court I had instructions to oppose such an application if it arose. I did not do so because it was not advertised, and therefore could not be heard.

James Cameron, Town Clerk, and Clerk of Court, looked at me over his half moon specs and said –

"Dickie MacKintosh"

I hated being called "Dickie." I always felt I was being put down when so addressed. Too true.

"Dickie MacKintosh. Before you cri'icise me, be sure of y'r fac's."

He handed me copies of the Herald and Chronicle which carried adverts. including Tom's, which I sought to oppose.

I was sunk. He had followed the letter of the law. My objection was incompetent. Whatever I thought of the reasoning behind James' ploy, I could not express.

In the absence of any valid objection the application was granted, and I determined in future to be "sure of my fac's."

MARRIAGE OF PRIVATE JOHN

In Scotland, according to Common Law, marriage could be constituted by consent alone, and if the parties were minors (over 16 and under 21) without parental approval. The Inverness Courier reported a case in 1831, of a young couple who arose in church, and in audible voices declared they were married. The paper added "Such public recognition is, we believe, binding in the Law of Scotland, and constitutes a lawful marriage." True

Since 1757 minors in England required parental consent, and regular celebration. The differing laws gave rise to the Gretna Green marriages – elopement to Scotland to gain the privilege of its more liberal laws. Prior to 1939 irregular marriages in Scotland were constituted by declaration, and we solicitors found ourselves conducting marriages in the office. This stirred up great excitement among the typing staff, who went to enormous pains to glimpse the bride, to assess her looks and attire, and whether there was any compulsitor on the parties to wed consequent on prior indiscretion.

The parties signed a declaration "I X, do hereby accept Y as my wife," and "I Y do hereby accept X as my husband. And we both declare ourselves married, the one to the other." "Signed, dated, and witnessed."

This alone would have sufficed, but society so often requires official proof of marriage by registration. So the parties appeared before a Sheriff who granted warrant to register, and that was it.

In 1939 irregular marriage by declaration was swept away, and the registrar himself was authorised to conduct the ceremony, after banns called in church, or posted at the registrar's office for fourteen days.

The act also provided that in special circumstances where fourteen days' notice could not be given, the Sheriff could grant a licence for the marriage, when satisfied there was a substantial cause for failure to publish notice. The most common cause was that of a serviceman posted abroad at short notice.

With the licence and two witnesses, the registrar performed the ceremony. Johnny was a private in the Camerons. He appeared in the Sheriff Clerk's office on a Saturday morning in 1956 saying he wanted to be married right away, because he was being posted to Aden on the Monday. A professional soldier seeking a professional shoulder.

The Sheriff Clerk phoned me at home at 10a.m. I met the couple in my office. They were both eighteen years of age – so young. We petitioned the Sheriff and presented it to an Honorary to obtain the licence by 11a.m. I told John to go to the registrar with two witnesses. He was expected. He had no witnesses. The Sheriff Clerk and I had to take the parts of witnesses. There was no ring, but that was not vital. It could be purchased in the afternoon.

Then the awkward question of payment was raised by Johnny. I asked him if he had any money, and he said he had a little. The going rate was £7:7/– so I suggested he let me have £2, which he did. We went our separate ways.

At 12.3- p.m. my door bell rang at home. It was Johnny.

"I'm sorry, but I haven't got enough money to buy the ring."

He got his £2 back.

Two years later a small parcel was delivered for me by hand – a beautiful pair of goatskin slippers, and a slip of paper bearing the word Johnny. I wonder who Johnny was.

MAKE A WILL

I knew Simon for many years. He was shepherd on the home farm of an estate I factored. He was a widower, without a family, without a will. The only relative was a half sister (same mother) Ann, a middle aged lady, and a spinster. There was an estate of £2000.

Among the papers Ann delivered was Simon's birth certificate, and her own, which was in short form, disclosing only the name and place of birth. I ordered a full extract from the registrar, and found that unbeknown to her, she was illegitimate. The estate would go to the Crown, as she did not qualify to inherit. (It's different now.)

It was not pleasant imparting this information to one who was deeply religious, but it had to be done. Ann manifested the feelings of one suddenly bereaved, and I felt guilty, without cause.

So H.M. Exchequer had to be informed – Simon was without heirs.

A Gentleman rejoicing in the title of Queen's And Lord Treasurer's Remembrancer became the automatic executor, and asked me to obtain Confirmation (Probate), in his name. This done, I uplifted the estate, and forwarded the proceeds to him.

Then it was necessary to pause for a year, after which a petition was lodged with the Q. and L.T.R. for the gift of the estate to Ann – entirely at his discretion. Without delay Ann received the whole estate.

So don't let us criticise this section of the Civil Service.

As an apprentice, I remember being advised by an ancient lawyer who must have been at least forty -

"Never draw a will containing a bequest to yourself, however small, and however much the client may feel indebted to you. Nothing is more calculated to make the name of the lawyer stink."

An old lady, Mrs. M. came to see me after her lawyer Donald C. died. She said she had been Donald's client for many years, but she did not like his surviving partner, and wanted a change. She put a bundle of titles on my desk, and asked me to take over her affairs, and make a new will.

"And how do you wish to leave your estate now?" I asked.

"To my man of business."

"And who is your man of business?"

"You are now, of course."

"You mean you want me to be your executor?"

"Yes, and I want you to have everything I possess, now that Donald's gone."

"I'm sorry Mrs. M. but I cannot act on that basis."

"You mean you won't do it?"

She left with her titles, and in a bit of a tizzy.

A week later she phones me to say not to worry. She had been to see another lawyer S, whom I didn't like very much, and she left everything to him.

She died within the year. I wasn't interested in how much she left, but I was curious enough to inspect the will and confirmation in the Sheriff Clerk's office. His register is a public one. S did the will. S did the administration. S got the lot.

Volumes are left out of the Ten Commandments. If I were S, I could not but walk the streets with bowed head.

In making a will, I resisted sheer vindictiveness on the part of the testator, and also I disliked it when the instructions were given in the presence of a "friend." Often I had the question – "What do you think I should do?" That one I evaded. Once or twice a relative who felt he did not get his just dues, regarded me as a guilty party.

One such person, a maiden lady of untender years, who had occasion to call in connection with the administration of her brother's estate, used to bring in baggies of tablet, which she gave to my secretary to spite me. I enjoyed that.

Banks make wills and act as executor. It is a good selling point that banks never die. When K died I found his banker had made his will. Everything went to his wife, who was to be joint executor with the bank. Fair enough. But there were three teenage children. The bank ruled that one third of the moveable estate should be retained by the executors against possible claims by the children up to the age of 25 for their legal rights. This was a severe handicap to the widow in meeting the costs of educating her children. It would have been gentlemanly if the bank declined office, leaving the widow access to funds, and to take the risk definitely remote, of such claims. As it was, she was in the hands of complete strangers, and obliged to visit head office when she wanted to consult. Oppressive.

I speak of one bank only. Others, thank goodness, did not behave so.

Equally oppressive is the cost of a funeral.

When I was young, there were few parents who did not protect themselves and their offspring with "penny a week" policies of insurance, designed to defray funeral expenses should need arise. The amount of cover then, was £22. This indicates soberly, that then as now, they very thought of a "pauper's" grave, like the Poorhouse, struck terror in the hearts of the poor, and not so poor.

It is judged vital to a family that a deceased member should have "decent burial." It is the "right thing to do." Failure would horrify the neighbours, disgrace the distant relatives, condemn the family to irredeemable obloquy. Tradition, the practice of ages, the influence of superstition and mythology, all affirmed the certainty – we must conform. Vain wisdom and false philosophy. Worry, worry, worry.

To unleash the fetters of centuries is no easy task.

And what the reward? The liberation of a host of sufferers from the soul destroying worry of the cost of dying. It is positive as illness. It is illness. It should be treated as illness. The trouble is that it is a secret illness.

Let's cut the cost of death. Who will give the lead?

What about recyclable coffins? This would not affect the delicacy of the religious service. It would slash timber imports. Let's use cars instead of limousines, hatchbacks instead of hearses.

Once only did I witness a burial at sea. The remains were sewn into a hessian envelope. The deceased was honoured, and the service in keeping. It could not have been more compassionate.

To what purpose do we inter with the mortal remains, the expensive trappings of convention?

Please do not infer I am knocking our funeral undertakers. They do what the consumer wants, and in my experience, do it kindly, with efficiency, and dignity. They would probably be the first to agree that if customs changed, so also would they.

It is fairly well known that when a person is blind or unable to write, the will can be signed by a solicitor or the Parish Minister, provided it is read over and understood by the testator. A banker friend asked me to have a will signed on behalf of an old lady in hospital. She was unknown to me. He said he had prepared the will himself, because it was very simple. At the hospital, I concluded the old lady was incapable of comprehending what it was all about. So I refused to execute. In terms of the will the whole estate was to be left to the banker's two sons. I lost a friend, but with no tears. And I was angry. No more work came from his bank.

P was a real tearaway lawyer, who told me this story when he was in ripe old age. It could be said he took a wee dram. Truer to say he took an almighty bucket.

He was taking instructions from a contemporary for the preparation of a will. At the end of the interview the testator said -

"And one last thing. I want you, after the Minister is finished with me at the graveside, to sprinkle a bottle of Glenfiddich into the grave. I've lived happily with it all my life, and it might be a comfort in death too"

My friend thought of the diabolical wanton waste of it, and asked thoughtfully -

"Would you mind if before I do this, I first strain it through my kidneys?"

THE FIRE (4)

Duncan complained -

"It's now two bloody years since the fire started, and we are still not in court. I just don't think you have been doing your stuff, and I'm fed up with you and your excuses

"I warned you at the outset of the time scale. In fact I'm surprised you did not start bellyaching before now. If you want to change your agent I won't complain. But before you do so, I suggest you take home my correspondence file and read it."

"This sounds like more of your soft soaping, and I'm sick of it. I'll take the file, and I'll be back to you soon."

Away he went with the file. I didn't want to abandon his case. I was totally immersed in it. Though we had the occasional slanging match, I had a profound admiration for this man who was prepared to take on British Rail single handed, something at least another dozen lairds had shrunk from doing.

The court granted access to the engine sheds, and to the staff and records of B.R., Forestry Commission, and the War Department. British Rail appealed, and lost. This exercise consumed nine months of Duncan's two "bloody" years.

All witness statements taken to date were sent to Counsel. Rose's was masterful. He covered loss of profits, damage to woodland, sporting, road surfaces, bridges, fences, culverts, drainage, contingent loss of capital, and injurious affection. The Belgian engineers found eighteen engines without spark arresters, and two with suppressors a year old and worn out. All in all it looked like a pretty good case.

Our Edinburgh correspondents advised B.R. intended to make this a test case, and would fight all the way. The thought occurred to me this might be a swipe at our morale.

B.R. suggested we try to limit proof by agreeing the question of damage. We corresponded and met on this subject, but our views were so disparate, we gave up. It was futile trying to negotiate, when they intended to compromise in no way.

Duncan brought back my file. He conceded me nothing, but made no further mention of sacking me.

Counsel, a Q.C. asked for a consultation.

I told Duncan I knew Counsel quite well. We were in classes together and I employed him several times as a Junior. I looked forward to a pleasant meeting.

Duncan and I went to Edinburgh together, and called at Counsel's chambers, in a large gracious house in the New Town. A maid showed us in to a huge dining room, in the centre of which was a vast oval table. We sat at one end, and waited fully twenty minutes. Then the great man made a pompous and theatrical entrance, with our brief in his hand, and seated himself at the far end of the table. The warm greeting I expected did not materialise. How he had changed. There wasn't even a hand shake, and no sign of recognition of one who had fed him quite a lot of business, when he badly needed it. He was corpulent and florid faced. Not a sign of a smile.

He pronounced – "This case is nearing proof."

He didn't need to tell me that. He fingered the papers in his hand

"I see you have precognitions from....

He named our witnesses.

"Do you think they will stand up to the testimony in the precognitions?"

I thought that a pretty stupid question, and broke in -

"Will you tell us please what is your estimate of our chances?"

Then he entered the blustering wool-over-eyes act – "if...and if...and if."

By this time I was real mad.. Clearly, he knew nothing about the case.

He had not read the papers.

I brought the consultation to an end, and thanked him for his time. He was glad to be rid of us.

Outside in the street once again, Duncan was fuming, as I was.

"We'll have to get shut of that bastard," said Duncan through his anger.

"Don't be too hasty, Duncan. Let's give it time, and we'll think about it."

He liked his food, and he gave me a good meal in l'Aperitif.

COMPANY NOTEPAPER

I mentioned the bustle there was to form new companies in the immediate post war years.

Major X conceived the idea there was an opening for a high class tailor, "bespoke" was the term. He had in mind a first class London tailor with highland origins to manage, and a big secret – he had a source from which he could obtain clothing coupons, for we were still in rationing. He reckoned a company would provide limited liability. Safe as houses. It did not occur to him his banker would require personal guarantees for overdraft.

I formed his company.

The prestige of the house, would require to be emphasised by the eminence of the directorate. He enrolled General K, Major General L and Col. M.

At the first meeting of the company, discussion turned to the format of the notepaper and bill heads to be used. Major X said -

"At the top left hand will be a heading 'Directors.' Underneath -

Major X Chairman.

General K

Major General L and

Col. M

Then there will be a new heading – 'Secretary." He turned to the lawyer -

"And how shall we design you, Mac?"

The lawyer's reply was -

"Able Seaman."

The company went bust within three years.

MOUTH TO MOUTH

Emily retired from presiding over the sub post office counter, where she made herself ever so popular over a period of thirty years. She was determined to enjoy her retirement, now that her ailing mother had passed on, and she had time on her hands.

She called to see me, and Shirley at Reception said -

"Yes Miss Emily. I'll see if he is free."

It was at this moment Emily felt her head begin to swim. Her knees sagged, and she gently fell to the threadbare carpet. The contents of her hand bag were disgorged alongside her. She uttered not a word. Shirley's scream alerted her room mate Rhoda, who called me to the scene. Bob Mactaggart our accountant forestalled me. We crouched down alongside Emily on the floor.

"Rhoda – 999 for Ambulance. Heart attack. Oxygen."

Bob ripped off the scarf and unbuttoned the coat. I felt the skirt tight and didn't know how to loosen it off. I cut the waistband. The face had gone ashen white, with a tinge of blue.

With Emily on her back, Bob thumped the rib cage once or twice and then commenced mouth to mouth. He had the neck in his left hand and I pinched her nose, while he opened her mouth and blew. Her bottom dentures fell out, and he cast them aside impatiently.

Nothing was happening.

Blow, pause, pause, blow.

I took her wrist in my free hand. No pulse.

Bob probably did not realise that that between blows he was muttering

"C'm on, y' booger. C'm on y' booger."

"Pump again." Bob told me. Pump, one, two, three. Pump, one, two, three.

Something told me, maybe something I read – don't overdo the pumping I stopped and took the wrist again.

"Towels Rhoda. Wipe the mouth. Stuff that lot back in her bag. Wrap the teeth in a Kleenex."

Blow, pause. Blow, pause.

Three minutes. Five. Seven.

"Something's happening," I told Bob when I felt an ever so slight movement of the pulse.

"Thank Goad," said Bob. "We'll carry on for a wee while to see if she will open her eyes."

Emily flinched, as though to escape the treatment. The eyes opened.

"Towels, Rhoda," Bob shouted.

Just in time.

"She's going to spew."

Bob had her turned on her side, and the towels arrived just in time to catch the vomit.

The recovery seemed miraculous.

"What am I doing here?"

"You just had a wee turn. You'll be all right soon," said Bob. "We're sending you to hospital for a check up."

She noticed a small area of spillage on the lawyer's carpet, and wanted to wipe it up. Fancy doing that to the lawyer's carpet!

The ambulance arrived and she was taken to Raigmore Hospital. In four days, like a good trooper, she was out and about as right as rain.

She had no recollection of anything that happened. We never told her.

I fetched a bottle of whisky, and gave Bob a mouthwash. I had a little too, and so had Rhoda. It gave her the giggles.

THE SMITH

I knew him from early boyhood, the Smith.

He wasn't a big man, but the arms and shoulders were those of an ox. How often I watched as a boy, fascinated, as he flattened flat strips of iron on his anvil, sparks flashing in all directions. And when I fell in the river, it was to his forge I went to get dried off and save a beating at home,

He came to me from time to time for advice, to collect debt, and to have a will made.

But he was never so worried as when he came to report he was losing money. He was busy, but he had no money. He couldn't understand it. It was agreed Bob Mactaggart and I should go to the smiddy of an evening, and examine the books. It wasn't difficult to find what was going on. Biro pens, when first introduced were taboo with banks and lawyers, but gradually, they came to be accepted. There was a tiny office tucked at the back of the smiddy, and Cathy, a presentable sixteen year old, was employed to keep the books there. She wrote out the cheques, and the Smith signed with a biro. With each heavy handed signature, the cheque below was indented, so that the lines of the pen could be easily followed. That's what Cathy was doing. We told him to sack Cathy the following day, and took the books away with all returned cheques and stubbs, to find out how much was missing. It amounted to £1000.

We wrote the girl's parents. They at first denied everything, but gave up at the mention of the word "Police." At a stretch, they could find £300. We went to the bank, who made no bones about admitting their liability. They had passed cheques which were forged. So we recovered the lot, and the bank paid expenses, on the basis that the Smith's account continued with them.

That was the Smith's great adventure.

Eventually, he retired, and had time to yarn. He told me of his young days in Patagonia. Many young men from these parts went, before the First War, to be sheep farmers in Patagonia, where horses were used extensively on the farms. He worked as a Smith, and collected numerous trophies for his skills. No-one could match him for shoeing. I was intensely interested. But in time he became repetitive, and a bit wearisome, as retired men are inclined to be. I know. I am one. So, I tended to avoid the Smith because he had so much time, and I had so little. How true that in the end every hero becomes a bore.

When he died, his daughter, whom I knew quite well, brought his papers to me, to attend to his executory. I told her how much I enjoyed his stories about Patagonia.

"What," she said, "My father was never further from Inverness that the Keith show."

MRS. DRUMMOND OF THE TRAVELLING PEOPLE

Mrs. Drummond was one of the Travelling people, the matriarch of her tribe.

She came to me for help in the autumn. Her family had taken occupation of the vacant Seafield House in the Longman, and the Town Council as owners, wanted them out.

Her first question was – "C'n the hornies (Police) pit us oot?"

My answer was – "No, but you have no right to be there, and you know that."

"Och aye. Bit we only want t' stay t' the spring. C'n y' no do that f'r us?"

I took to this old wife with the gnarled, smoke-browned face, the wee slanting eyes, and the black teeth. I had heard of her before, for her progeny had made frequent appearances in court, and struck the local press. She could make a statement in mitigation as good as any lawyer, and she was likely to be believed. I had heard also of the anger in the Town Council about the squatters in Seafield House, and the ineptitude of the Council employees who failed to make it secure.

"I can't guarantee to keep you there till the spring, but I may be able to help a little. Sometime soon you'll get a paper from the Town Clerk asking you to quit. When it comes, bring it to me."

Two weeks later, she called again and handed me a service copy Writ for the ejection of her and her family, signed by the Town Clerk, James Cameron.

I asked – "Can you read?"

"A wee bittee."

"Do you know what this says?"

"Och aye. The Cooncil want us oot."

"You know they have a right to put you oot?"

"Och aye. Bit if you're worth y'r salt y' c'n put them off till the spring. Anyway, the fermer said we could come in f'r a night. That was before a left himsel. It's going t' be a caul winter. It's a sair thing naebidy likes tinkers."

"I don't believe that. It's only that they don't understand you."

I said I wanted to see Seafield House, and went there next day on my bike. I was met by four raucous hounds, mongrels all, barking their heads off. I was too petrified to run for it, so I placed my bike between me and the dogs, while they continued their racket like a battery of guns. Close by a garron grazed peacefully, not in the least disturbed by the dogs.

I felt a bit odd, in my new demob suit, and natty trilby.

Mrs Drummond came to the door.

"Hush y'r gulder."

That silenced the dogs, who then became quite friendly.

"C'm un. The kettle's on."

She took me in to the roon to the right of the door. There was a bright fire in the iron grate. The fuel seemed to be floorboards. An iron kettle sat on the hob, a puff of steam rising lazily from the spout. There was an old fashioned girdle to one side of the fire. Of furniture, there was none, but several wooden boxes served as chairs. A few blanket rolls against a wall represented beds. The bare floor boards were scrupulously clean and fresh smelling. It was even cosy. I was invited to sit on a box at one side of the fire. My eyes roved over the drab wall paper, at several points stripped, hanging loose, Garlands of neglect.

We talked until she felt the tea had stewed enough. She poured a stroopach of real black tea. The heavy china cup looked perfectly clean, though minus a handle. No milk. No sugar. It was like drinking raw whisky, which no man can despise. Then she put half of a quarter bannock of oat cake into my hand, dry. It was good. I saw the girdle served well.

Towards the end of our talk, I said if I was to help her, she had to help me, by keeping the peace at Seafield – no brawling, no shouting, no drunkenness, and no need for Police interference.

"Dinna fash y'r sel laddie. I'll see t' that. We'll no sconce (tease) the hornies, an' I'll no let the men get soused (drunk) here."

As I departed, I got a glimpse of the room on the other side of the front door. No floorboards. Not even joists. Just bare earth.

Back at the office I lodged a Notice of Appearance in answer to the Writ served on Mrs. Drummond.

When news reached him, my friend James Cameron phoned, angry.

"What the hell are you up to? You know you have no defence."

"Ah ha!" thought I. "I shall put one over on James in response to the demolition job he did on me in the liquor court."

"We'll see."

The point of service to the point of proof in a civil action could be up to six months. I sought to spin it out. In these days Sheriff Grant was pretty liberal with "continuations," on the most flimsy of excuses.

Mrs. Drummond called on me for progress reports from time to time, and became quite a favourite with the staff, principally because, living as she was indoors, she did not stink of wood smoke.

At last, by the end of March, I told her no more could be done.

"Ach, that's all right laddie. Ah kept m' promise t' you, an y' did no bad. Ah've nothing to greet over. We'll be oot in a week. Y'll no see us for stoor."

I intimated abandonment of the defence.

James obtained decree against Mrs. Drummond, by which time she had departed.

Some weeks later I met her on the Suspension Bridge. She moved the short stemmed clay pipe from the corner of her mouth smiling like to crack all the wrinkles. She greeted me like a long lost.

"We're fine now. We've got a graan camp below Torvean, near the canaal. Here – tek this reenge f'r y'r wife."

From the big square basket on her left arm she extracted and handed me a heather pot scrubber.

I was enriched by this

THE LAND COURT – BELIEVE IT OR NOT

I knew the Land Court best when Lord Gibson presided.

Appearing for a landlord, your chances were minimal. Appearing for a tenant you were half way home before starting.

Gibson tried to hide but could not obscure his ignorance of agriculture.

His greatest love was Gibson, and it was ill concealed.

The court was itinerant, travelling the country to hear cases close to the loci of the disputes. He revelled in wearing his regalia – crimson robe with large white ermine crosses, wig. The lawyers always carried wellie boots for the inspection of the holding which followed the hearing.

His lordship was supported by a legal assessor, who was a qualified lawyer, and acted as Clerk of Court, and buttressed also by two technical advisers, lay members, experienced farmers.

I have attended hearings in conventional courts, in public halls, in a Town Hall, in schools, and in hotels. And out of doors in summer sometimes sitting on the grass, and in winter standing shivering in coat and gloves.

Frequently hearings took place in the croft kitchen, when his lordship for practical reasons, graciously dispensed with his regalia.

I recollect a sitting in a croft kitchen at Dochfour, when first the lady crofter was asked to chase hens out, and later proceedings were halted to remove a pet ewe baying outside the window.

The lady of the croft usually, and with an eye to pleasing, provided tea and scones, which his lordship affably accepted to demonstrate he had the common touch. Besides, he enjoyed it.

The dignity, combined with the informality of a hearing in the kitchen was a phenomenon to be seen to be believed. The canary hung by the window, the collie lay before the fire, and the cats begged for a bite when tea was up. When the light failed there were oil lamps and candles. An air of comedy? Yes, but it worked.

By any standard, the court was peculiar. It was also often amusing. Would that its official records disclosed that side.

In Lewis there was a dispute between crofter and laird about a march fence, alleged to be defective.

"It's jist aaful," deponed the crofter. "Ah canna keep ma stock unn. Ut's deplorable what ah hev to' pit up with. Y'll see for yersel. There's not a strand o' wire less than thirty year old, an' th' posts th' same. As f'r strainers – they wouldn't hold a hen. Only last night one o' ma best ewes, ah havena got many, but thus wis one o' ma best, an' pure bred, dud she no get through th' fence an' away she was down th' rodd t' Stornoway. Anytheen could hev happened t' her, anytheen at aal. It was Goad's mercy ut wasna ma wife that was unn it."

In Skye the court was due to sit in a remote village school, an occasion warranting a holiday for the pupils. An adjoining crofter, part time janitor, was instructed on his duties – to be in attendance when the court assembled, and stand by while it sat. Of the two rooms, one was to accommodate the court, and the smaller one was to be the judge's retiring room. The janitor, who had never before been involved in such an important duty was understandably nervous.

Minutes before assembly he saw a wee man in a bowler hat and black coat, carrying an attache case approach and walk into the school. A tax man, thought the janitor.

Minutes later the "Tax man" appeared resplendent in wig and gown. The janny was flabbergasted. Never had he see such an apparition. He could be forgiven for intoning -

"Good Goad!"

"Yes," said the great judge, patting him on the shoulder. "But strictly incognito."

On another occasion I was trying to obtain an increase in rent of a farm which seemed radically undervalued for rental purposes. I was summing up, and in full flight when I heard a loud, discordant, gravelly, chest deep snore. Judges do not usually snore in my experience – sleep, but not snore. I halted, and asked the senior lay member – "What do I do now?"

"Don't worry. Carry on. We can handle this."

The result was quite satisfactory to me.

But you couldn't always have such luck. I was asked by the factor of Kyllachy Estate to act for the laird in a claim by a tenant crofter for reduction of rent. The basis of the claim was that the Findhorn river in flood had washed the top soil off an arable field. I asked to see the damage beforehand, and the factor said it could best be viewed from an elevated estate road leading to Clune, and on the opposite side of the river to the croft.

We took this road and the field was pointed out to me. I looked down through powerful binoculars and saw the area was covered in lush green grass. Obviously nature had reinstated the damage. So it would be a cakewalk.

The court convened on the holding.

There I saw long grasses on the field, but each stalk was no closer than eighteen inches from its nearest neighbour.

My case was in tatters before we started.

Walking the croft after the hearing, the judge buttonholed me and said -

"You didn't do your homework properly this time Mister Lawyer."

"No, my lord. I did not."

My degradation was somewhat mitigated. His lordship and I, straggling far behind the lay members, in inspecting the holding, encountered a five wired fence, with barb on top, too high to straddle with safety. The alternative was a long walk round. Raleigh like, I took off my burberry and spread it over the barbs, allowing the great man spang the fence without risk to vital parts. How very delighted he was with such a simple device, which apparently he had never seen before.

Coming back from a hearing in Portree with a friend on a summer evening, we found on reaching Kyleakin the boat was on the other side. While waiting, we took a stroll down the pier, where a ferryman was waiting to tend the ropes of the incoming boat. My friend noticed a number of high poles, like telegraph poles, ranged along the pier. On enquiring of the ferryman what was their purpose, my friend was told – for lights. On a very dark winter's night, the boat on a private hire was returning carrying guests from a dance in Kyle. A big wave lifted her high and she came down bashing her gunnel on the pier. The boat turned over and all the passengers were toppled into the water. So the ferry skipper said he must have lights.

"Och," said my friend, "They would all have been drunk."
"Not at aal," said the ferryman indignantly. "Waan or two of them waas sober."
Finally, a case which to me was an unhappy one. I was acting for a landlord in a renunciation of lease by a widowed crofter too old to continue. In her younger days she saw the potential of her croft for bed and breakfast. Over the years she prospered, and made many improvements – a beautiful porch to the front door, another almost as pleasing to the back, an extension providing two extra bedrooms, a picture window, a large bay window, elaborate coloured cement pathways, a brick garage for two cars.

The widow lady was entitled to compensation at outgo for any improvements effected during the tenancy. But I had to point out the compensation included only improvements "suitable to the croft." The items I mentioned could hardly be considered within that category, so the valuation discounted them, and the landlord obtained a smart little modernised cottage for next to nothing, which he promptly sold for an excellent price.

I was sorry to have to plead such a case. The laird didn't need the money.

It was a pity land court work did not yield a better return to the lawyer. It had to be faded out in consequence, except for special cases.

NIGGLING LAWYERS

Most lawyers were conscious there were some among them who niggled.

The firm of Y's in Glasgow was one such. In buying, no title seemed to be good enough for them. Without warning they would retain 15% of the purchase price, against satisfaction of an insignificant point of title or boundaries. Vexatious behaviour. They were just infuriating people. I truly wondered whether their object was to nettle the other lawyer rather than to benefit their client. Fortunately, this was not the norm in conveyancing transactions. Usually the two lawyers sought to co-operate to achieve the goal they both aimed for.

So when I was handling the sale of a north west coast estate close by a fishing village, and where there was also an hotel, I was depressed to find a client of Y's was the highest bidder. I had to be on my mettle.

While indicating preparedness to agree their offer, before closing the bargain, I sent them the titles, saying it was a condition of sale that these titles were acceptable. I also provided settlement would be by way of bank transfer, and only when the transfer was effected would the keys of the hotel be delivered and the conveyance handed over to their local representative.

The manageress of the hotel, Celia, a wise and loyal one, and quite tough too, was advised that on no account should her keys be delivered until advised by me. She would not open the hotel or pub on the morning of settlement.

When the time came, bank transfer was effected, but 15% of the price withheld. Why? because it was found an adjoining proprietor was crossing the north end of the subjects to reach his fishings on a loch mutually owned. Answer – the adjoining proprietor has no title giving him such access, but he had been a good friend, and no exception had been taken. If Y's were not satisfied, they could interdict him – but they might like to keep in mind he was the Lord Lieutenant. There was also a bleat about the boundary at one point. The title rested on a plan on the six inch scale, with a thick red line demarking the boundary, and such a plan could not delineate boundaries with mathematical precision.

The phones began to buzz.

Celia rang. She had a demand for the keys.

Answer – "Tell them you have no authority. Please lock all doors and close all windows."

Y's phoned. They had a right to withhold. We had not given them what they had contracted for.

Answer – "We disagree. Release the cash, or no entry."

Y's – "We shall raise an action and force your hand."

Answer – "You are welcome."

I was in a secure position. I had learned Y's had sold on the hotel, so that other agents, like me, were giving them hell, for not delivering the hotel keys.

Celia again – "It's nearly eleven o'clock when the pub should open. What do I do?

Answer – "Nothing."

Celia, later – "There's a gang of fishermen hammering on the door for me to open up."

Answer – "How many?"

Celia – "About twenty."

Answer – "Have you plenty of draft beer?"

Celia – "No, I've run it down."

Answer – "Have you beer in pint bottles?"

Celia – "Yes."

Answer – "Give the fisher boys a bottle each on the house, and say we are doing our best to get organised. Serve through a window. Nobody to get into the premises."

Y's – "You are causing chaos at the hotel. We shall have a claim against you for loss of trade, and costs consequent on delayed settlement. Stocks have arrived at the premises and the manageress will not accept them."

Answer – "These are your problems."

Y's a good deal later – "We are prepared to pay you 5% from the sum retained."

Answer – "Not interested."

Y's still a good deal later – "We have transferred the balance of the purchase price."

Answer – "We'll check."

The bank told me that payment was received in full, and I told Celia to release the keys.

Y's – "We are told you gave free beer to the fishermen, and after stock-taking. It didn't belong to you. You will have to reimburse us."

Answer – "Take a running jump."

It was a joy to put a noose around the necks of these people who constantly caused trouble unnecessarily over the years.

Three months later I saw a notice in the Law Journal that Mr Z of Y's whom I recognised as my adversary, had retired from the firm of Y's, to take up an appointment in the Procurator Fiscal's service. He should have enough opportunity there to exercise his aggression. And maybe Y's developed better relations.

"Oppen uup!"

THE FIRE (5)

Usually, I did not require to ask Duncan for a call – he had been haunting me for over two years. This time, the meeting was at my request.

"Have you sacked that sod we met in Edinburgh?"

"I've thought about it, but my answer is 'No.' Despite his treatment of us, he is a very clever man, and he has a reputation to maintain. By any standards, yours is a very prestigious case to fight. Potentially, it can make legal history. I want to stay with him meantime."

"You surprise me. I don't have much option but to accept your advice. But I tell you, if he makes a balls of it, I'll have your guts...... What did you want to tell me?"

I handed him a letter from my Edinburgh correspondents. B.R. sacked their legal adviser. Any further negotiations would be conducted by their Area Manager.

"Where does that take us?"

"Good Lord! Don't you see, this is the first blink of sunshine since we started on this case? You know Lumsden? He is a reasonable man. We may get somewhere with him. He has already phoned me asking for a meeting."

"Well, Let's get on with it."

"It's no use going to a meeting without deciding tactics. We're suing for £x and you have run up about £3000 in expenses. Lumsden will want an all in figure. We have to keep in mind the amount will be £3000 less in your pocket. Rose's figure of £x as you well know, is pretty highly pitched. We can afford to come down. What do you say?"

"£X – y."

"And that is the least you will accept?"

"Yes."

"Right. I'll phone."

Lumsden asked – "Can you come round now?"

It was a short walk to his office, and we were shown in to his room without delay. I knew him quite well. He was formal, perhaps I thought a little anxious. But he was my no means hostile.

"I am prepared to admit," he said, "that this case was not very well handled by our people up to the present. I have authority to settle, and I am not going to argue with you, because my figure, in my view, represents a very fair offer. So, you can take it or leave it. If you agree, I'll give you a cheque now. If you do not, I'll instruct our Counsel to intimate a tender for that amount to the court, and you know what that means."

I knew. If we succeeded in court, and the amount awarded was less than the sum tendered, we should have to meet expenses. I explained this to Duncan, and asked Lumsden – "As we have nothing to lose, what is your figure?"

"£X – z."

This was £5,000 more than Duncan and I had as our minimum

I looked at Duncan. Duncan looked at me. I nodded. Duncan nodded.

I said I would write out a receipt giving the company a complete discharge. This I had signed by Duncan and I passed it over the table. In return Duncan received a cheque for £X – z.

Gone went the tension. All three of us were beaming. We parted with Lumsden the best of friends.

Duncan, though elated, could not believe the business had come to so sudden an end, and would not until he saw the cash credited to his bank account.. He insisted on calling on his bank manager to pay in the cheque.

The manager sent a clerk to the rail bank nearby to be cleared, which it was. Duncan saw it at the credit of his account.

He was now over the moon. "We've got to celebrate," he said.

We went to the top town hotel. He ordered a bottle of the most expensive champagne.

I said – "What about asking Lumsden to join us?"

I phoned Lumsden. He was most grateful, but said if certain people saw us together, wrong conclusions might be drawn. It was too risky. I said I was sorry, and I hope we might have another chance at a later date.

"Glad it's over?" I asked Duncan.

"I'm not complaining about the settlement."

I said – "We got there in the end, although we had some hairy moments."

"Well," said Duncan, "I wouldn't want a bloody 'Yes man' for a lawyer."

WALTER'S PRIME INVESTMENT

The laird was becoming old and infirm. He couldn't stalk, fish, or walk his grouse moor.

He decided to pack up, but he had the decency to take account of his tenants. He had valuations prepared of all the holdings on the estate, and then made offers to sell to the tenants. Having regard to the "tenant in occupation" effect on the valuations, and the discounting in addition, each tenant was offered a snip. Eight bought. That left only Walter.

Walter never believed any good could come from landlords or their Factors. Anything to make himself awkward to the landlord was done by Walter. There was timber on his hill, but it had been sold to a merchant, and was excluded from his valuation.

I begged Walter to buy for his own sake, but he did not expect reason from a Factor. He was the kind of man who took forever to make up his mind about little things. To become a landlord in his own right would be a momentous move.

He was a great one for taking advice, at the mart, in the pub, at the shinty, and even after the kirk service. In the course of a year the weight of advice was beginning to wear him down. Then I put pistol to his head – buy within a month, or the offer to sell would be withdrawn, not to be renewed. I was getting fed up. If he wouldn't buy I could sell to a speculator at a higher price.

He agreed verbally to buy.

As though to celebrate the occasion, Walter tried to clean his chimney by sticking up a load of old newspapers, and setting them alight.

The soot fired all right, but so also did the house. The Fire Brigade managed to restrict damage to the kitchen, parlour, and bedroom. As the property had not formally changed hands, the estate insurance company paid for reinstatement. Walter got a beautiful new kitchen, parlour, and bedroom.

The sale went through.

Within a year the time limit for felling imposed on the timber merchant expired, and the contract was therefore at an end. The bottom had fallen out of the timber market, and it became uneconomic to extract. The standing timber reverted to Walter.

Within another two years, up went the market again to dizzy heights. Walter sold for a handsome price. So he obtained his farm free of charge, with a bit in his bank as well.

I have pondered on the moral of this story, and I don't know if there is one.

In any case, I was quite happy Walter had such good fortune. He wasn't a bad sort really – just awkward. Soon after, he married a very nice lady, of whom I thoroughly approved, and they were well pleased with each other. I don't know how long Walter took making up his mind to marry, but conceivably his brilliant land deal was a help. It sure gave him something to boast about at the mart. He walked even taller than his six feet two.

CONVEYANCING ODDITIES

Look back to the last century. Donald Jack had a property in King Street, adjacent to a vacant site, leased to Kenneth Beaton. Kenneth had no plans for his site, and would be quite pleased if Donald could use it. When Donald was paying his feu duty to Major Huntly Duff of Muirtown, he asked to be given the vacant site. Duff took up his quill and penned a conveyance -

"Here goes in a crack

"Kenny's site to Donald Jack.

H.R. Duff."

The title was found to be valid. I applaud the brevity. I am sceptical of its efficacy in today's context.

An instance of the utility of the feudal system. A builder obtained a feu from our Provost, Jimmie Grigor, and undertook to erect a specific number of houses within a specified time. The custom then was that purchasers paid the prices by instalments, as building progressed. At a stage when several purchasers had paid two or three instalments, but were still without titles, the builder went bankrupt. The Trustee in bankruptcy rightly claimed the whole building site with all structures reverted to him. The various purchasers would be claimants on the bankrupt estate only for the instalments they had paid. They stood to lose heavily. It was a disaster. At this stage, the Provost stepped in as Superior, saying either the Trustee would grant titles giving credit for all instalments, or he would repossess the whole site as it stood, on the ground that the builder had failed to complete the development within the time prescribed. The Trustee was forced to accept the lesser of two evils. The purchasers obtained their titles without loss, and completed their houses themselves. A bank must have suffered, but banks have broad shoulders. Don't let's always decry the wicked superior.

Nairnside estate was owned by English Trustees, who held on behalf of a liferenter, and on his death, for other members of family. There was a large area of ground on the estate suitable for housing development, and the liferenter sought to feu for that purpose to augment his income. But English Trustees have no power to feu. Suppose they did so irrespective? Who were the interested parties? Only the Trustees, the liferenter, and the subsequent heirs. The first two as parties to the transaction could be ruled out. The subsequent heirs were eventually to benefit from the enhanced income produced. They certainly could not lose.

Suppose we ran into any trouble with any solicitors who spotted the problem? A guarantee of title could be obtained from an insurance company.

We went ahead, and gave off dozens of feus. Dozens of solicitors inspected the title for their clients, including the toughest cookies in Inverness, and, believe it or not, Messrs Y's of Glasgow. Not one questioned the right of English Trustees to feu. And after the elapse of ten years from the grant of feu, the title became unchallengeable. Why accept an impasse when a common sense route can be round around it, hurting nobody, and benefitting many?

Mrs. F was an old lady who decided to give up her house and go into an old folks home. She had little idea of house values, and with her mind on the past, conceived the idea that £3000 would be a good price. An "Estate Agent" came into the picture, and she agreed his suggestion if he could get a price in excess of £3000, his fee would be the difference. He found someone willing to pay £4000, at which stage Mrs. F came to the lawyer. There was no written agreement between Mrs F and the agent – not that that would have made much difference. The proposition was monstrous. I acted for Mrs. F in the conveyance, and paid him £60 for his services, with an invitation to sue for the balance. He did not, but his business closed down soon after.

Another ploy of the "Agent" was to find dry rot or wet rot in a house he sought to buy. There could not be a more forceful compulsitor on the seller to get rid of his property pronto.

I had a country client who wanted to erect a kit house for summer letting. He completed a bargain with an "Estate Agent" and received his statement of account. I didn't like it. On enquiry at the manufacturers, I found the purchaser was entitled to 10% discount, not shown on the statement. One page, the last one of the manufacturer's contract, was removed before signature. That page contained the reference to discount. The "Estate Agent" lost his agency.

SOOPLE AND THE GREENBACKS

I inherited Soople as a client. He was charged with stealing £15 from his friend Mopie in a scuffle outside a pub after closing.

He pleaded "Not Guilty."

Mopie, a Merchant Seaman, was home on leave.

At the trial I was cross examining Mopie, when a note was passed in front of my nose. I looked around and saw the donor was my old friend J.C., at one time devoted denizen of the courts, and a star performer. He had abandoned court work some years before, and probably called in after a visit to the Sheriff Clerk. He wanted to see what was going on in his old battleground. The note read – "See notes produced. Brown. Union Bank. This bloke paid in Newcastle – probably greenbacks."

Right into my barrow.

"Mr. Mopie, did you leave your ship at Newcastle on the morning of the alleged theft?"

"Yes."

"And did you receive your pay on leaving the ship?"

"Yes."

"Was it part of that pay which you say was stolen?"

"Yes."

"And now you are on leave from your ship again?"

"Yes."

"And you came north yesterday."

"Yes."

"And you were paid at Newcastle before you came north on this occasion?"

"Yes."

"Do you have in your pocket any of the notes you received as pay yesterday?"

"Yes."

"Show them to the court."

Mopie fished in his breast pocket and produced a wallet, from which he extracted several notes.

"Will you confirm these notes are green in colour?"

"Yes."

"How come the notes you say were stolen are brown?"

The Fiscal deserted the case.

"*Any greenbacks?*"

A LITTLE BAG OF GEMS

Michael Ewan was a Chartered Accountant who ran a city practice single handed.

Among his clientele was a wealthy old lady who depended upon him for the management of her finances. She was more than pleased with the attentiveness he displayed in so doing. When she died the whole estate fell to Ewan.

He set about putting the money to work. One or two property deals paid handsomely, but his speciality was small businesses. He had a nose for finding young men building promising businesses, but retarded by lack of finance and business know-how. His policy was to proposition such men by offering financial help, on the basis they agreed to form companies in which he held substantial blocks of shares, and of which he became Director and Accountant. In effect, he could make others work for him. That was not dishonest – it was shrewd. And it was fruitful. He successfully manipulated a bakery, a nursery garden, a cafe, a general grocery store, and factories making concrete blocks and system built houses. There was no problem about pulling out handsomely rewarded, for his co-directors usually regarded him as a growing incubus to be discarded at any cost. Nobody likes being milked.In the mid 1930's he made a point of meeting the young twins who were modestly advertising Radical Radios. They bought, sold, and maintained second hand "wireless" sets. We would contemptuously call them steam radios, a mystery of valves, and wires, to the uninitiated, simple as pie to the savant. They were driven by a big clumsy expensive dry battery, renewable about once in four months, and an "accumulator" – a wet battery rechargeable about once in three weeks.

Business boomed. A company was formed.

Ewan wanted to open a town centre retail shop, which the twins regarded as premature. In the impasse, a Special General Meeting voted Ewan, Director and Accountant, out.

He had no option but to seek a sale for his shares, but a sale required the consent of the twins.

The accounts prepared without Ewan's help, for the second year of trading, showed a substantial loss, a result which Ewan thought impossible. He considered the offer made by the twins for his shares derisory, and the antagonists found themselves in court.

The solicitors involved were McLeach, no hum dinger, for Ewan, and Jacobson a top notcher in company law for the twins. Ewan was completely out-manoeuvred. He lost the case and a lot of money.

This unhappy experience gave Ewan to think he should have a smart solicitor. His business went to Jacobson, who brought him into big time – hotels, public houses, cinemas, and dance halls. It was a hectic life, but nothing seemed to go wrong. Hard, hard work, an obsession with money and the capital mounted.

Ewan's wife died, but for years absorbed in business concerns, he had been seeing very little of her anyway.

He had a daughter in her thirties, teaching in an English boarding school. If he had an affection for anyone, it was for his daughter Sarah, whom he called Sal.

As the year 1938 dragged into 1939, Ewan and Jacobson contemplated what effect an eventual war would have on Ewan's riches. A few visits to associates in the world of depressed finance in London, persuaded Jacobson to advise that Ewan go into industrial diamonds in a big way. Thus it was that Ewan possessed £100,000 in uncut diamonds, which he kept very carefully, in a modern safe at home, a safe which had both a key and a combination lock.

Sarah was told of this purchase. He gave her a copy of the secret numbers in the combination, and showed her the secret drawer in his desk where the key was kept. He showed her the linen bag which held the gems.

The war came, and dragged on.

Returning by train from a business visit to London in August 1944, Ewan died of a heart attack. The only paper in his possession identifying him with a third party, was a letter from Jacobson, who was therefore the first connection to be advised, by a phone call from the station master at Mortpark.

I had been acting as local correspondent for Mark Perant, a middle ranking partner in a Glasgow firm. I had occasion to visit him in Glasgow early in 1946. He asked me if I knew Ewan. I said I did not, but I had heard a bit about him. We discussed the man for a little, and after some fencing, this is what he told me.

"I act for Sarah Ewan. She told me that immediately he received the call from the station master, Jacobson drove to Ewan's home. The housekeeper was shocked to learn of her master's death. She knew Jacobson quite well as Ewan's solicitor, and she gave him access to his study, "to collect papers." He said he was the executor. He was in the study for about half an hour alone, and left carrying was appeared to be correspondence. After the funeral he read the will to Sarah. It was simple – the whole to Sarah, and Jacobson the executor. Until that stage Sarah was too upset to think of the contents of the safe. It was several days later she unlocked it and applied the combination.

The bag which contained the diamonds was not there. 'What could I do,?' she asked. 'I wrote Jacobson to confirm the diamonds were in his possession. He said he was not aware my father owned any diamonds.' I later advised Sarah she could raise an action against Jacobson, but the chances of success were negligible. He wasn't the type to be affected by conscience.

I took Counsel's opinion, but no joy.

Have you any ideas?"

I was sickened that a solicitor could behave so, but saw no solution. The diamond market, unlike the stamp market, was not one in which a seller or a buyer operating carefully, could possibly be traced.

Jacobson took eighteen months to complete the administration of Ewan's estate. He had his business account taxed by the Auditor of Court, his executory account audited by a qualified C.A., his own discharge as Executor prepared. Sarah refused to sign. He withheld settlement with her until she did.

Then he retired.

ANENT INSURANCE

No-one would contest that insurance is important. Most would admit that insurance people are very agreeable to deal with.

Until a claim arises.

Then the company imports an assessor to negotiate the claim. He is an expert in his narrow field. He can convince you, for this reason and that, you are not entitled to receive the full amount of your claim. In case of fire, you are underinsured, though your figure is up to market value, replacement value is another matter. On replacement, you will also enjoy "betterment," which has to be discounted. You never took into account the cost of demolition, if required, and clearance of the site. And of course, there will be architect's fees. As to contents – what about that oil painting auntie Jean left you? Is it valuable – is it covered? Keep in mind you bought a music centre three years ago, and a video this year. Covered?

You are in fact in a jungle. What to do? Obviously, do it before disaster strikes. You've never read the policy? The type is too small. Get an independent expert to go over the policy with you to tell you what is in and what is out. It's worth his fee. When the fire comes, it's too late.

If you have a claim for personal injury – do you know the worth of an eye, or a leg, or a finger, or an arm? The assessor does. He's right up to date on court awards. Your lawyer isn't, because his court cases are two or three years out of date. Your lawyer is not a specialist. The assessor can make rings round the provincial lawyer.

The toughest people I've had to deal with were Lloyds, a name hallowed as the world's leaders in maritime insurance. Their arguments were endless, and the time they took to agree a figure unconscionable. There was then unexplained delay in settling, giving the remote country lawyer timorously to suspect the object was to hold off, to get the maximum use of your money in interest before parting. Such experiences point to the propriety of dealing with companies who have proven track records. Those offering the lowest premiums seldom meet that criterion. The easiest claim to have settled is on a life policy when you die. Good thing too. You are in no position to argue.

My firm, in the early days, had an excellent relationship with a Scottish company. All our disposable business went to them, and we were on cordial terms with their Managing Director, and Head Office staff. Top level decisions were obtained quickly, and the best possible advice received on insurance affairs, both at Head Office and local levels. The inevitable happened. They were swallowed up by a massive English company. We became chicken feed. We lost the service to which we were accustomed. We even had to resort to, horror of horrors, to reading the policies.

One of the most interesting characters I met in the field of insurance was Walter Crane, an independent assessor, much employed by insurance companies. He was a mature man, old enough to have participated in the First War, in which he lost a leg. He seemed to manage quite well with a cork replacement. He came out of the infantry with the rank of Captain, and an M.C. To my knowledge, he never used his rank or title. In a number of cases I used him for my own business purposes, to vet and report on vehicles, preliminary to action for breach of warranty. He proved an excellent witness in court, and stood tall in my estimation.

Despite my admiration for him, I began to notice when his name cropped up in conversation with some of my older associates, my respect did not seem to be shared, and I wondered. I had a client a well-to-do farmer who held some fields on the periphery of the town. From time to time he let out these fields as "bed and breakfast" for stock brought in for disposal at the auction mart.

I raised the name of Crane at a meeting with him, he was silent.

Next time he called he showed me a letter from Crane addressed to him and dated in 1935.

The letter contained a request for the use of a field for a rally of the British Union of Fascists.

ADOPTION

There was quite a demand for adoption petitions to be presented to the Sheriff. Most of these originated with the Children's Officer, a very dear senior lady of the Public Assistance Department of the Town Council. Most of these petitions went through uncontested, but I struck trouble in one case where the child was placed by a City Adoption Agency.

A delightful young couple took the child into their home for the usual three months trial prior to petition. They became very attached. When the petition was presented, the natural mother claimed to have changed her mind, and refused consent. My people were distraught. I decided to contest the case, thinking that, in the private hearing which would ensue, I might be able to persuade the natural mother back to her original resolution.

The lady supervisor of the adoption agency was required to give evidence, for I regarded her, in reality, the guilty party. In the event, she refused, on the ground she had a prior engagement to give a talk to a group from a women's organisation. Of that, I took a poor view, so I cited her formally, and she couldn't refuse.

The object of the case was to decide what was best for the child, having regard to accepted principle, that in the absence of good cause, a child should be in the custody of the natural mother.

I did not shake the natural mother in cross examination, and had to accept in my own mind, she had a genuine change of heart.

The child was returned whence he came.

For the proposed adopting parents, it was a tragedy, but happily my friend the Children's Officer soon arranged another adoption, which turned out completely successful.

EXHUMATION

My first experience of exhumation was at the instance of the American War Graves Commission. It was their policy at the end of the War, to return the bodies of all American servicemen buried in this country.

Exhumation required the authority of the Sheriff, and if he were satisfied on the grounds of the application, he directed the act to be carried out under the supervision of the Medical Officer of Health and/or the Sanitary Inspector. I never required to attend any of these exhumations, my function being solely to obtain authority. As the interments had taken place only three to five years previously, the caskets were still in quite good shape, so that the operations were reasonably clean.

Outside this series of cases, I had only one experience of exhumation.

A very old lady, whom we shall call Mrs. Smith, died in a country district and I arranged the funeral, with the nearest undertaker, leaving him to instruct the opening of the grave, as was the custom. She had no living relatives, and insufficient funds to meet the cost of an ordinary funeral. Only two or three attended, and all was completed very quietly.

There were many families named Smith in the locality, and a responsible (and meddlesome?) citizen alleged the lady had been interred in the wrong grave. On making enquiries, this was found to be true. Had no action been taken, probably no harm would have been done, for the family who originally owned the lair used, had also completely died out. But there was a complaint, and nothing for it but to assuage local feeling.

The Sheriff was petitioned and an order obtained.

The Verger opened the two graves which were within fifteen feet of each other.

With the undertaker, the Sanitary Inspector, and his assistant, I attended at the graveyard.

We simply raised the coffin by its original cords, and walked it to and lowered it into the correct grave.

There was no religious ceremony.

I think it left us all with a queer feeling.

CONFIRMATION – POST HASTE

In the administration of executrices, one of the most frustrating delays was caused in the Sheriff Clerk's office. When the Inventory of Estate was lodged with him, all detail of the estate had to be typed on to the confirmation form. There was a constant bottle neck. The Sheriff Clerk attributed this to shortage of staff. I thought a substantial contribution was made by a lazy and very senior clerkess.

An administration takes long enough without this kind of delay, adding fuel.

In my own office we solved the problem by arranging with the clerkess concerned that we ourselves would type the confirmation form. She then simply checked our typing against the inventory, and arranged for issue of confirmation. Unorthodox, but, when the devil drives.

These were the days before photo-copiers.

MacKellar, like many of his co-solicitors, chided at the time taken to issue confirmation.

A wealthy client of his was in a terminal illness. He had complete control over the client's affairs for some years, and in the will he was the first name executor. Beforehand, he had arranged a text case with the co-operation of the Sheriff Clerk, and a friend in the Estate Duty office in Edinburgh. The client died one morning at 4 a.m. At 8.30 a.m. Mac was on the train to Edinburgh, with a completed Inventory of estate. He called on his friend in the Estate Duty office. Duty was assessed and paid. He arrived back at base in the evening. By appointment he called on the Sheriff Clerk, and delivered the inventory, and the pre-typed confirmation form. The Sheriff Clerk completed confirmation, and delivered it on payment of his dues.

This stage was reached within one day – three days before the funeral. The circumstances of the case were all favourable to the tactics employed.

One day will never be the norm. The Sheriff Clerk insisted on a quid pro quo. Under the Sheriff Principal as Returning Officer, the Clerk was responsible for the organisation of Parliamentary Elections within the County. He always had difficulty in finding responsible persons to act as presiding officers in remote parts of the County. He reckoned lawyers were capable of reading, understanding, and implementing their instructions. He favoured the appointment of lawyers.

MacKellar, having readily agreed to the penalty, accepted appointment in Kinlochmoidart, dropping and picking up ballot boxes at all Polling Stations en route. Well, he didn't get paid very much, but he had quite a lot of fun.

THE FIRE (6)

It was five years after the fire.

Duncan called with his current problem – Capital Gains Tax. But that is another story.

I was pleased to inform him I had read in the Scotsman that British Rail was introducing diesel engines on all lines where fire hazard existed.

I suggested – "You can take a bow."

He was not moved, but I think it gave him some satisfaction. It certainly enhanced his status among his peers.

It was July – the run up to the grouse season.

I asked – "Is there any increase in your grouse stock this year?"

"I've never seen so many birds in all my life.

CAPITAL GAINS

I hate tax. I hate tax law.

But I couldn't completely ignore it.

There were times when points arose in tax law which the accountants could not answer. Almost always when such points were put to me, I couldn't answer either.

It was Duncan our friend of the moor fire who put this one to me. He had a talent for making life difficult.

His father had been the liferenter of a substantial landed estate in the south west coast. When the father died, the estate, with extensive agricultural and forestry interest, was released to Duncan. He managed it for a year or two, but at a range of two hundred miles he found it a bit of a bind, and thought of selling. It was 1965.

"Will I have to pay Capital Gains tax?"

"I don't know."

"Well, you're the bloody lawyer. Why don't you know?"

"It's not the first time I told you 'I don't know,' so you need not get het up about it. I'll investigate and come back to you."

I had heard of Capital Gains, but had read nothing of it. I knew is was introduced by a Socialist government, and that it therefore was bound to swipe at Duncan.

To me, reading a Finance Act is like reading a foreign language. The draughtsmen have to be so careful, almost every statement is fenced with – "ifs," and "but," "provided," and "subject tos."

I went back to the office to work in the peace of an evening. Before long, my head was swimming, and I hadn't got a grip. I gave up. I went back to it a second time, and parts were beginning to make sense.

Then I came on a clause which seemed to me to say that on a sale, if the purchase price, is re-invested in comparable business assets, exemption would be enjoyed. Applying this to Duncan, if he re-invested the purchase price in his home territory, where forestry and agriculture were major components, he would be exempt. But I wasn't over the moon – I wasn't sure. What I read of tax law often didn't mean what I thought it did. Back to Duncan.

I asked – "If you sell, what do you propose to do with the proceeds?"

"Never thought about it. I suppose there would be too much to drink."

"Don't give me that crap. You have a lot to say about drink, but I never saw you drunk, and I don't think you drink all that much. This is a serious business. I want to know what you will do with the purchase price."

"Why is that important? What do you want me to do with it? Can't I do what I like?"

"It's important because, if you were to invest it in your estate in this side of the country, you might be exempt."

"But, you're not sure?"

"No. I'm not sure, but if you tell me you'll plough it in here, I would like to go a stage further."

"O.K. Let's say I'll do that."

"Right, I've found a clause in the act which seems to me to support my view. But, with tax, you never know what view the Inspector will take. I would like to go to see the Inspector to try to get confirmation. He is under no obligation to advise on what is at the moment merely a hypothetical case."

I went to see the Inspector. I had met him before, and thought he was a reasonable man.

I put my question and he answered – "I don't know."

Blimey! What now?

But he added, "Let's see if there is anything in my guidance notes which would help. It's an intriguing question."He dug out a very fat paperback, and thumbed through it, with many references to the index. Fully half an hour he spent on it, till at last he said – "I can't find anything. I'll get on to Lothian Road and ask them there."

Lothian Road in Edinburgh housed the Chief Inspector of Taxes for Scotland.

It was agreed he do that, and come back to me.

A few days later he phoned. Head Office had agreed my view.

I asked him tentatively if he would be prepared to write outlining the view he would take.

"Certainly."

He was indeed a gentleman.

I received his letter the following day, containing what I wanted.

How wrong was my previous view that the tax man was but the custodian of tax about to be confiscated.

The proposition put to the Inspector is now called "Roll Over." Everybody knows about it. Not a big deal after all.

After this experience of taxation I thought I was going to have a rest from it. Not so.

Torquil was youngish, cheerful, and a very outgoing man who owned an estate not far from that of Duncan. His education was thanks to a revered English public school, more noted for its prestige than scholastic achievements. Through his school connections, he had friends in the London financial scene.

They knew how to avoid Capital Taxes, and readily advised.

In great glee he dropped on my desk a long letter from a London Finance House, advising how, if he wanted to sell his property, he could do so without paying these stupid taxes.

From my practical point of view, I was required to convey his estate to a company in Jersey, who would hold as his nominee. Like a Disposition in Trust, this would attract a stamp duty of only 50p. The interest of the nominee company was to be manipulated by assignation of reversionary interests and letters of authority through another two offshore companies, to enable Torquil vicariously to sell, immune. My suspicions were aroused when the London whiz kids organising the romp, tried to put it over that each case they handled had to be tailored individually, hence the colossal fees proposed. Then there was a monumental urgency to complete all moves by the coming 5th April, by which time the government would probably step in to remedy a lacuna in the law.

I could not understand the reasoning, and demanded more information.

I was sent an Opinion by an English Barrister, confirming the scheme was feasible.

Still, I was not satisfied, but under pressure from Torquil, I prepared and stamped the conveyance, but did not record. By recording he would be finally committed.

Meantime I persuaded Torquil to allow me to obtain Opinion of Counsel in Scotland.

53

We went to an eminent advocate known to me to be at the very top of his profession and a leading expert in tax law. One who went far since.

The opinion held the scheme would not work.

Torquil was sad, but he agreed to abandon to my great relief, and the chagrin of the London boys.

I was so very sure that once committed, Torquil would have lost control of his estate, and would be taken to the cleaners by a bunch of charlatans. How much did I understand the various arguments deployed? Not much so far as the English Opinion was concerned. A little more on the Scots one.

Preserve me from taxation.

PLANNING MISTAKES

In 1959 Town and Country Planning was in its infancy, and that is when, much delayed, the Inverness Town Plan was published.

The proprietors of Kenneth Street didn't like some of its proposals. The stated intention was to acquire most of the front gardens of the houses, to provide a sixty-four feet carriageway to this part of the A9 the road to the north.

For years these proprietors had been complaining of the noise, and danger of heavy, fast traffic, the hazard of exhaust fumes, vibration. Now it was proposed that this traffic be brought six feet closer to their houses. Their front doors would open to the street. Their values would plunge.

The enquiry into the development plan held in the Town House in May and June 1961 involving several wigs and gowns, lasted two weeks. That was the time it took to send the architects back to their drawing boards to think again. Kenneth Street and various other areas were saved from the destructive hand of the planners.

When the development on the south side of Bridge Street was under consideration, many thought it should remain unbuilt, and a grassy bank substituted, as a frontage to the castle. What distinction that would add to the town centre. No. The land was far too valuable to remain undeveloped. How short sighted. Had that been done the cost would be written off by now.

A model of the proposed development was made available for public inspection. The artistry of the model must have been superb. Many thought it delightful. Reality came otherwise. The layman cannot see with the eyes of the visionary.

So many planning blunders have been made in this beautiful town, they make you weep.

Experience has been expensive, but thank goodness it is a good teacher, and development is now in more delicate hands.

The solicitor plays his part in development, but not always in the best interests of the citizenry. He has to plead the case of his client, not of the commonalty. Pity.

THE SPOUSES BREAK-UP

She was short and plump, within an ace of fat, somewhat mitigated by a good complexion and hair-do, combined with a garish sartorial elegance. Her accent had no roots, and was patently designed to impart that she was top drawer. But, off guard, or in anger, she reverted to "pewer" Inverness.

If I found redeeming features they would be expressed. The harridan! I detested her whining and whinging, which never stopped.

She was married within her original station to Pat, a skilled house decorator, unassuming and severely hen pecked. My affection for Pat was in inverse ratio to my aversion for his wife Kate. Together they had consulted me over a period of a few years on various matters involving house purchase.

Then she came to see me by herself for advice on divorce. She had nothing but contempt for her husband. He gave her no children – I thought she was too selfish to have any. She could not bear to sleep in the same room as him. His only interest was to spend Saturday evenings drinking beer with the boys. He was common. They were constantly rowing.

Scornfully she told me he made a mock attempt at suicide by hanging himself on a coat hook on the back of the bedroom door. There was no dash of pity.

"The hook broke. Ha, ha, ha. People who say they are going to commit suicide never do," she pontificated. "I wish he would."

I advised nothing she told me constituted grounds for divorce. She was being stupid.

"Return to Pat. Encourage him back to the way he was when you married him, and compromise a little to give a fair wind to reconciliation."

It wasn't good enough advice for her. She had found another boyfriend, a building contractor, who treated her like a lady. If I wasn't going to help her get a divorce, she would find somebody who would.

I said – "If that's what you wish, do so. It's not for me."

Three days later Pat jumped into the harbour. He was not a swimmer. For a long time I wondered if I should feel guilt. I certainly felt a great sorrow.

INSOLVENCY

It's a funny kind of word. Why don't we say – "inability to pay debts?" Maybe it's neater the other way.

Robert Maxwell brought insolvency to the peak of notoriety, and escaped. Fortunately there are few achievers in that bracket, and certainly there never have been to my knowledge, in Inverness. But all who find themselves in this sorry state are not necessarily deviants. Like a ship's compass, the extent of deviation depends on the course. In the straight and narrow, there is none.

The causes of insolvency alternative to the crooked, include bad management, bad judgement, or a knock from the iniquities of others.

When Brain Inglis visited with his accountant, probably all these had influence. Brian was a young, intelligent, industrious electrician, in business on his own account. Each year his turnover increased, and success is a heady wine. Financed by his bank he undertook contracts he was well able to fulfil. But he was not able to ensure timeous payment from customers. He was under capitalised. The crunch came when a major builder for whom he was sub-contracting, failed. Preliminary estimates indicated that the builder's creditors would receive little more than a shilling in the pound. Brian was out on a limb. His bank was pressing. His suppliers were intolerant. How true, he learned, that a company in liquidation has no soul to save or backside to kick.

What to do?

The accountant suggested he stop trading immediately, and sign a Trust Deed. This was a means by which Brian would transfer all his assets to a Trustee, who would realise and distribute the proceeds proportionally to creditors. The banker agreed to this procedure on the basis that all creditors assented. Brian was confident he could find a job, and was prepared to pay to the Trustee a portion of his earnings.

The advantage of the Trust Deed was that it involved less expense, formality, and hassle than sequestration or bankruptcy (synonymous terms) and elided interference by the court.

The Accountant Jim Elder agreed to act as Trustee on Brian's assurance he would co-operate to the maximum.

It was necessary to call a meeting of creditors, and nearly all attended. Some were represented by solicitors. Some were really angry about their losses, and were out for blood. The solicitors subjected Brian to a rigorous questioning. He really was humiliated. Grudgingly the creditors agreed to the appointment of Elder, on the basis that Brian was not allowed off the hook. He was to contribute to the fund all he earned in excess of £X. He was to be left with a meagre living for two years. I have noticed that meetings of creditors usually generate a high head of steam. After they are over, the creditors miraculously quieten down, accepting their misfortune, and taking little further interest.

Elder commenced collecting outstanding accounts and selling assets. He met various unforeseen obstacles which caused lengthy delays. Brian did get a job readily, but did not take well to working for a boss. He sought relief in drink, a perfidious companion. His wife left him.

Needless to say most of his creditors became aware of the changed circumstances.

The local Bank Manager, on reporting to Head Office, received instructions to take steps to petition the court for sequestration. This was competent despite the existence of the Trust Deed, which was superseded by the action in court.

Everything now became very formal and very complicated, and very expensive. The bank's solicitor blew the dust off his copy of the standard work – Goudy on Bankruptcy, and followed step by step in accord with the instructions of the learned and long deceased Goudy.

Seven years passed before Brian obtained his discharge, by which time he had sobered, and became resigned to his lot. He continued to work for a master, which gave him a good living, without the kudos of being a contractor.

It was his best friend who told him the secret of contentment is to realise your own limitations.

THE KIRK PUB

"Jimmy, where's Eilean Fluch?"

The question was posed by Alex. Ness, recently appointed Clerk to the Justices of the Peace – public spirited men who adjudicated on applications for Liquor Licences.

"Never been there," replied his assistant Jimmy Weir, "but I believe it's an island ten miles off the north west of Skye. A launch serves once a week from Uig, weather permitting. That's the only link with civilisation."

"How many inhabitants?"

"I suppose there may be about two to three hundred. Male adults are crofters or estate workers – shepherds and stalkers – and of course they fish. They have the best prawns and lobsters in the north. Trouble is marketing. There's a tin shed Kirk which functions when they can get a minister, and serves as a one teacher school, the nurses clinic and the Ceilidh Centre. And I remember hearing somewhere they have a great tradition for piping, fiddling, and harping. They call the harp the clarsach."

"Well," said the Clerk, "I've an application here to the March Court for a public house licence at 2 ½ Eilean Fluch. That's a funny address, 2 ½."

"It's not funny in the west. Only means a stance has been split. Good luck to them. They could probably do with a little more diversion."

How was either to know 2 ½ was in fact the tin shed – the Kirk?

The Clerk went through the usual procedure of advertising the application, and inviting objections. As ever the applications were scrutinised by the conventional objectors. The licensed trade saw no competition, and therefore no reason to object. The Police were obliged to inspect, but it was their practice to check on weather before approaching the island. Their contact was by radio telephone with Mackay MacDougall, who, among many other duties, acted as Postmaster. Each time they phoned him he said – "Ach, man, Y' know the March weather. We've an aaful heavy swell. Y'couldn't get ashore."

So the Police did not inspect, nor did the Presbytery of the Kirk, for the same reason. It was not in the interest of any residents to object. We shall see why.

Mackay MacDougall, of ancient fishing stock, risked his life to attend the County Licensing Court on the mainland. He read a statement in support of his application – a statement couched in terms which tended to indicate composition by a more erudite mind.

The basis of the case was that Eilean Fluch was an isolated community, clinging to a traditional way of life in desperate conditions. The only hope of remaining in the land of their fathers was to develop the tourist industry. Tourists were entitled to expect at least the minimum facilities in the islands, which included a dram. Nobody wanted to see St Kilda re-enacted at Eilean Fluch. The way Mackay put it over tore at the heartstrings.

But there were facts unknown to the Court.

Two years previously Eilean Fluch got a new laird, and a new Minister, full time. The Laird was Campbell Clark, director of a distilling company, and wealthy. The Minister was Gordon Graham, talented, but poor, a half brother of Campbell.

Campbell Clark called the householders to a meeting in the tin Kirk.

"I have a proposition to put to you. If you modernise your houses you can get a 50% grant from the County Council. I will put up the other 50% as interest free loans repayable over five years. Then you can take in summer guests and make some real money."

"But," said Mackay, "we canna get people to come heer without advertiseen an' that. We canna afford that kin o' money."

"Leave that to me," said the laird.

So it came to pass that every able bodied householder had plans prepared by the Minister for modernisation and/or extension of their houses, and these were approved for grants.

Campbell instructed a Glasgow firm of developers. A workforce of fifty men, all experienced tradesmen, were landed, accommodated in a tented village, and served by professional caterers, who employed several locals.

Materials were delivered in bulk by large cargo vessels, off loaded to landing craft, and deposited at points on various beaches close to existing house sites. The whole community was fired by enthusiasm for the scheme, and freely provided unskilled labour. The workforce toiled from April to August, by which time the project was completed.

One night each week was devoted to recreation. The Kirk never knew such scenes. The fiddles, clarsachs, and pipes came our for the ceilidh, and there was dancing into the small hours.

Refreshments there were too, and at ridiculously reasonable prices. A band of willing volunteers recruited by Campbell converted water into wine, operating a small still, peat fired, in the open, in all weathers, throughout the preceding months. When not in use the still was sunk in a convenient lochan, suitably protected.

As soon as the liquor licence was confirmed it was time for the publicity. It was too easy. Clark leaked to the Press that on Eilean Fluch A LIQUOR LICENCE HAD BEEN GRANTED TO A KIRK. It was front page news in many of the nationals, and was eagerly featured in all regional newspapers. Enterprising news hounds found their way to Eilean Fluch, with photographers, and portrayed the modern but traditional housing, as well as the Kirk pub in the best possible light. BBC and Commercial Radio Stations intrigued by the comedy of the situation gave it big licks, and the TV cameras were quick to latch on to a story not without humour, and free from the conflicts which usually constitute news.

Inevitably some church people on the mainland felt obliged to be outraged by the idea of a licensed Kirk. They couldn't do much about it, because the building belonged to Campbell Clark, and he was subsidising the Minister's stipend. The huffing and puffing from church quarters soon died down.

The first season Eilean Fluch launched itself as a tourist centre "away from it all," every bed was booked from May to October.

The following year Clark built a new Kirk pub to a suitable vernacular design, and the Kirk used it, doubling the membership.

Sadly, it was necessary to abandon the "still" waters. That's what I was told, but I wouldn't know for sure.

PURCHASING THE MANSE

The manse belonged to Church A, and it was surplus to requirements.

I had a call from the Reverend of Church B, who said his session was interested in acquiring, but on no account was I to disclose the name of the interested party. If this were done Church A would refuse to sell, because Church A and Church B held differing views on fundamentals, and Church A would not willingly sell to Church B.

The recommendation to sell was put to the congregation of Church A, and they were willing sellers. But the property had to be advertised, and sale would be in the hands of H.L. & Co. Solicitors, Edinburgh. I was in contact with the Session Clerk of Church A, a gentleman of some distinction in the area, with whom I had established quite warm rapport. Naturally, he enquired the name of my client. I had to tell him that meantime, that would not be disclosed. He was disappointed, but not unduly upset.

Back to Church B, whom I advised it would be prudent to have a structural survey. This was done by a builder member of Church B, who reported, subject to minor detail, the manse was in good shape. Advertisements were placed, and eventually a closing date for offers was fixed.

This I reported to the Reverend, who was still very concerned that there be no disclosure of his interest. Were that to come to light, without doubt, Church A would not sell up to a competitor for the faithful in their congregation.

It was necessary to meet with the Session of Church B. At the meeting the vital concern was, non disclosure of interest. That point disposed of, by binding their solicitor (me) to the secrecy of the tomb, they proceeded to consider the amount to offer. I was surprised to learn they had in mind a very realistic figure, and one which I genuinely thought would succeed.

It then transpired that it would be a condition of acceptance that after sale, the title "Manse," would not be used in relation to the subjects, and no alcoholic liquors would be sold therein.

I put this to the Reverend, and he came back reporting that after consultation, these conditions would be quite acceptable.

So the offer was lodged, on behalf of an unnamed party.

Came a letter from the Session Clerk referring to the offer, and enquiring the identity of the offerer.

The Reverend said we could confirm it was not X, Y, or Z, but further we could not go.

H.L. & Co. said in the circumstances they proposed granting title by way of a feu disposition with a nominal feuduty. The title would preclude the sale of alcohol. There was also a buy back clause – a right of pre-emption – if Church B ever sought to sell.

I wrote to the Reverend reporting, and advising the conditions were unlikely to deter his Session in the purchase. He agreed.

The bargain was closed, and H.L. & Co. were advised we wished the title to be taken in the name of the Trustees. I asked the Reverend for the name of the Trustees. He names six, and said these would have to be intimated from the pulpit ten days before the Congregational Meeting. This was a worry to me. I told the Reverend these Trustees would eventually die off, and then there would be trouble with the title. I suggested the title be taken in the names of the Moderator, the Minister, the Session Clerk, and their successors in office ex officio.

The Reverend saw the sense in this suggestion, and it was agreed. He gave me a resolution of the Congregational Board appointing the office bearer Trustees.

There was a little difficulty in adjusting the boundaries of the ground to go with the manse, but this was easily settled.

H.L. & Co. eventually gave me a draft of the Feu Disposition, which I revised without much alteration. But now, I had to disclose the identity of the purchasers. I advised the Reverend the time had come, and I had to give the firmest of assurances the purchase would not fall through in consequence.

As a matter of courtesy I phoned the Session Clerk, apologetically advising the purchasers were Church B, regretting I was under strict instructions not to disclose this earlier, and hoping the transaction would not give rise to too much dissent within his church.

The reply was – "Doesn't matter a button to us. Good luck to them." Then he wrote the Reverend a very friendly letter, saying his people were very pleased he was the successful contender.

THE SORROWS OF A DEPUTY PROCURATOR FISCAL

In the late forties, I was a fairly frequent visitor to Portree – the Land Court, the criminal court, the Road Licensing Court. On criminal work my adversary there was Bill Paterson, a robust Fiscal, who gave no quarter, but who was fair. We became quite friendly. Bill was translated to Inverness around 1950, and wanted a deputy to function during his holiday periods or illness. He asked me to act. I did not fancy Fiscal work, but there were two considerations which influenced me to agree. First, since Bill was a stranger to Inverness, I could help him out in several ways. Second, in my youth I was always eager to gain experience, and it might not be a bad thing to see the criminal court as a prosecutor for a change.

A drawback was that I could not appear in the liquor court in my own parish. That was not too serious. I had partners free for that work. I was doing a fair amount of liquor court work outside Inverness, and the occasion arose when I had an application for a licence in Lochaber. The applicant was unknown to me, but he had reasonable testimonials, and Lochaber was a notoriously difficult area in which to obtain a new licence. So there were prospects of a good fight.

The first Licensing Magistrates' court presented some opposition, but not very effective, and the licence was granted. The case then required to be heard all over again by an Appeal or Confirmation Court. Through the grape vine I heard the big guns were to be arrayed against me. The opposition was represented by a solicitor, who elected to lead the evidence of witnesses, unusual in this court, where the custom was to base judgement on productions and submissions – letters supporting or antagonistic.

With foreknowledge of adversaries who would testify, I was able to frame well beforehand the basis of their cross examination. Those concerned were all prominent citizens, but for one reason or another, in my opinion, biased.

There were wheels within wheels here. Of this I was certain, but had no means of proving a vendetta had been set up by those with like interests. Divining rods were not required to point. The smell test sufficed. The public interest had no place.

I think the vigour with which they were attacked came as a surprise, and they felt affronted, all the more so as the public was well represented in court, as were the press. They had the satisfaction, however, of seeing my application refused.

A few days passed.

I had a call from a plain clothes Inspector of Police accompanied by a uniformed Sergeant. I knew them both well. We often exchanged banter. Not this time.

Said the Inspector – "Your full name is ... ."

"Yes."

"And your address is ... ."

"Yes."

"You have an appointment as Deputy Procurator Fiscal to the Sheriff Court here?"

"Yes."

By this time I tumbled. The poor Inspector was both nervous and unhappy. This job was not to his liking.

"As a Solicitor you represented ... ... in the Liquor licensing Court at Fort William on ... ..."

"Yes."

"Then I am going to charge you. You need not say anything, but anything you say ... ... I charge you that on .... while holding office as a Deputy Procurator Fiscal, you did appear as a solicitor acting in an application for a liquor licence at Fort William on .... contrary to Section ...."

"I have nothing to say."

I was not unduly worried. There were several solicitor Honorary Sheriff Substitutes, clerks to the liquor courts, part time fiscals, and deputy fiscals, constantly appearing in liquor courts throughout the Highlands, scatheless. Were I convicted there would be a complete turn-up of the book – storms galore.

My police friends left me without apologies explicitly ventilated, but manifestly implicit in their demeanour.

If not worried, I was at least cross. Here regenerated, was a repetition of the smell I got in Fort William. The concept of a prosecution had to be initiated by a coterie with some clout in the community. And they were nameless.

I told the story to Bill Paterson, concluding -

"I know of the statutory provision which supports the terms of the charge. I consider it to be desuetude. You know perhaps better than I do, it is flouted throughout the whole Highland area. If the charge was made to stick, believe me, I would create a most almighty stink, and liquor licensing in the Highlands would be crippled. I certainly did not expect this kind of treatment when I became your deputy, for which I am paid in peanuts."

It was unnecessary to plead a case to Bill. He was even more upset than I.

"I'll have a word with Crown Office," he said.

Next day he phoned.

"Crown Office tells me your point is not new. In 1944 when solicitors were even thinner on the ground than now, the then Lord Advocate issued an instruction to fiscals. They were not to prosecute under the Act in cases such as yours. The instruction still stands. When I get your papers from the Police, I shall mark them "No pro.""

TOM TO THE RESCUE

I liked Tom. He was a retired Marine Engineer, who did not believe in swimming against the tide. He was as simple soul who liked to give and receive a crack, dead pan.

Marrying late in life, he took his vivacious wife to the attractive house he had inherited from his father. His wife saw the house had a great potential for use in the bed and breakfast trade. Tom took no exception, but secretly resented the lack of privacy during the holiday season. As much to give his wife freedom in running her very successful business, as for his own comfort, he erected a small wooden shed in the garden, to constitute his retreat. There he had electric light and power, a couple of chairs, a bench, and his tools. In passing, I should mention there was a compartment in one of his tools boxes of the exact size of a standard bottle. When not absorbed making toys for his wife's church sale (He was neither practitioner nor believer), devouring the Daily Record, or filling in or checking his football coupon, he visited certain watering holes. These kept the right blends for his sophisticated palate, and he had his own corners by the bar, where he exchanged views in desultory fashion with like minded cronies. The quality of pensive repartee, determined quantity of spirits, which, let it be said, he held like a man.

Not invariably, but from time to time, it was his custom to take a short walk after the mid morning refreshment, to clear his head and prepare his digestion for the delightful meal his lady consistently served up for him.

It is on such a walk we meet Tom on a warm summer day. He crossed from the west to the east side of the river by the Suspension Bridge, and turned upstream by Castle Road, and Ness Bank. As always, he was enjoying his quiet meander. Past the War Memorial he went, and on to Ladies Walk, a footpath, traffic free.

Ahead of him he was vaguely conscious there were children playing in the river, in particular a group of ten year old girls wading, dresses packed into their pants.

One became detached from the group, and suddenly gave a piercing, terrified shriek – "HELP!"

Tom became alive. Banished was the haze of alcohol from the brain. Like a seaman of old, he tensed as he assessed the situation. Without thought for his own safety, he threw off his jacket, and half scrambled and half swam to the damsel in distress.

She was in six inches of water.

Tom to the rescue.

POD – VOTARY OF THE MARRIED STATE

Podmore was a shocker, a bluff Australian with a broad and ugly accent. He was a huge man, bloated and florid of face, and carrying the biggest of bellies. His constant companions were a couple of heavyweights as ugly as he, and approaching his own stature.

On arrival in the north he purchased a dairy farm and a gracious mansion, where he settled to live the life of a gentleman. Cash seemed to be plentiful.

He ingratiated himself with certain locals by his judicious and generous gifts to their charities, and represented himself as a tough, thrusting business man.

Where the fortune originally came from was a matter of conjecture, though there were whispers of trading in raw spirits, and even gun running.

He made numerous visits to London by Rolls – with bruisers escorting.

Unlike Pod, his wife was quite well liked among the shop keepers with whom she dealt. Always beautifully dressed, she had a kindly demeanour, to which the locals responded. She participated in no social activities, but it was understood she supported her husband when he entertained his business agents, which he did often and lavishly.

But Mrs. Pod wanted a divorce. She said he had an employee on his dairy farm, Mrs. Garter, with whom he was having an affair.

Clearly this would be dynamite.

Respectability was something Pod sought diligently. He would be unlikely to submit readily to conjugal attack.

Mrs Garter fell out in a big way with Pod. Were she to help Mrs Pod in a court action, it would put a knife into Pod's back, and give no mean satisfaction to a vindictive lady.

Mrs. Garter's statement was first class so far as it went, but corroboration was required, and in time was obtained.

Papers were sent to Edinburgh for Counsel to draft the Summons.

About this time Mrs. Garter took train for Edinburgh to visit a friend.

Around Pitlochry, while she sat alone in her carriage, Pod made a dramatic appearance, backed as usual by his shadows. He demanded that Garter leave the train with him. She refused. A struggle ensued, and she pulled the communication cord. The guard appeared and restored order. The Police came on board at Pitlochry, and escorted Pod and company off the train.

While making her way down Leith Walk in Edinburgh Mrs. Garter was waylaid by two men and bundled into a van.

She was not heard of again, nor was the divorce action.

Mrs Pod, now mysteriously incommunicado to me, said through her husband's agent, her husband would pay expenses to date, but he didn't. He was sued, and delayed right up to the day before the proof. The publicity of that he could not bear, even though the case against him was impossible to prove. So he did.

AILMENT AND INFLATION

At the age of nineteen Maud became pregnant. She consulted a solicitor to whom she alleged that Hendry was responsible. Hendry received a solicitor's letter, and he too consulted a solicitor..

The two solicitors negotiated.

For Hendry it was said there was little point in taking any action till the child was born, and at that stage blood tests could be taken in case they might be of help.

In due time, Maud had her child, a daughter.

Dr. T.M. Mac, Haematologist, was asked to take and analyse blood samples from both Hendry and the child. This he did, and reported the result proved negative. That meant that paternity was not disproved. Such tests were capable of proving Hendry was not the father, or Hendry could be the father, but not that Hendry was the father.

It was time for Hendry to think again.

He elected to pay up without admitting paternity. The lawyers were back on the scene. They agreed that the going rate at the time was 30/- per week. An agreement was completed, under which Hendry undertook to pay the sum for sixteen years on the basis that the child remained in Maud's custody over the period.

We were in the late sixties. Neither lawyer could foresee how this settlement would soon be affected so radically by runaway inflation.

Conceivably, Maud could have resorted to the court to have the amount of ailment raised to relate to inflation.

She did not do so.

DIANA – GODDESS OF THE HUNT

I am now going to describe to you a lady. She was no ordinary lady, so I must take it slowly and carefully, handicapped as I am lacking talent in the fine arts. Starting at ground level, she did not wear high heels as many do to give the impression of classical deportment. She did not require to. No London model walked with greater natural grace, straight in the back, square in the shoulders, head held high, with an ease redolent of a red deer in biped form. I've heard the carriage described as semi-military. I would say a little less, to exude an air of integrated femininity. The ankles, rounded and well proportioned supported on a pair of legs moulded to a paradigm excelling any revealed on page three. Usually the description of a lady does not include the bum, which is a mistake. She had a beautifully rounded but not too prominent pair of buttocks, topped by a surprisingly slim waist. Proceeding upwards, and to balance the buttocks, were two firm shapes, best viewed through a summer dress – especially in motion. The face was not that of a conventional beauty, but rather rounded, full lips and clean skin. I was never privileged with a close-up of the eyes. They looked sooty, half framed by medium heavy dark eyebrows. The hair, thick blonde, was quite close cut, and having a mild natural wave. And all this within a frame standing five feet six inches high.

Her name was Diana. Diana was the goddess of the hunt, a misnomer.

She did not have to hunt. She was hunted.

Right, let's leave Diana meantime. We'll come back to her.

There came a young man to this town well versed in tax and accountancy. He bore the name Monar, and lived happily with wife and two young children in an attractive stone built house. After a year or two the buzz went around the club that he was quite a ladies' man. Some whispered he sired a child to a waitress in an Edinburgh hotel, and others that he was the father of the baby of the shepherd's daughter at .... I can't remember where.

Currently he often burned the midnight oil in the office, enthusiast that he was for his work. And he had a winsome secretary.

He was employed by Matthew, our leading accountant, and able and good natured professional.

You're beginning to get the drift, so we return to Diana.

She felt the need to consult a lawyer. She had in any case been pushing a baby in a pram for at least three months, far more in pride than ignominy. But don't get me wrong. She did not flaunt her aberration. She bore it with dignity.

The story ran along these lines -

"Well it was like this. I was very friendly with his wife, and occasionally I did baby sitting to allow them to enjoy social occasions. I was on duty one night when she was attending a reunion, and he was to be away overnight on business. I got a bit of a shock when I heard the front door open about 9 p.m. and heard him call to his wife – 'I'm home.' The shock arose because the children were asleep and I was having a bath. I dried off, put on a dressing gown, and with a towel over my hair, went down to the lounge. He had taken off his jacket and tie, and was helping himself to a whisky. He seemed surprised to see me, and opened his arms to give me a kiss. I thought it was all in fun. When he held on to me, I knew it wasn't. And I found I was as much in the mood as he was.

He performed magnificently. I enjoyed it."

"So, what brings you to me?"

"He is not helping with the keep of the child. I would like a pound or two from him – not much, just enough to get me by. I asked him by phone, and he promised, but no more. I don't want to disgrace him – only frighten him, which I thought you might be able to do."

But Monar was not responsive, so he received a Writ. That galvanised him into action. Diana was content.

A day or two later I met Diana in the street with the baby.

"Look at him," she said, "Isn't he a pet?"

I had quite a start when I did peep. It was as though I was viewing Monar through the wrong end of a telescope. I mused that I had never heard of a baby being used as a production in a paternity case. If that "pet" was only momentarily viewed by the Sheriff, Diana's case would be made. Fortunately, it didn't come to that.

Inevitably the news reached the club. Diana raised an action but withdrew. The question was raised – does Matthew know anything about all this? No-one knew. Kenny, a contemporary of Matthew, and in the same profession, agreed to break the news. He did.

"What did he say?" was the question Kenny met when next in the club.

"He knew nothing of Monar's exploits."

"Was he angry?"

"Not really. He said 'Fancy that now. If I had known he was so talented, I would have put him out to stud."

Diana

THE KIRK HALL WALL

The Kirk Hall was in bad shape. There was dry rot in the roof, and the single brick wall which constituted the east gable, was crumbling. I had often heard from builders that Elgin brick was sub-standard. This was a good example. Bad firing was given as the cause. It had stood for a hundred years. Even so, it should not become ruinous so soon.

The Deacon's Court took the bit between the teeth. There were practical men in their number. The only solution was to rebuild the hall. A fund was started. They could have made an immediate start to rebuild by borrowing. That was not their style. They had to have sufficient in the kitty to meet the cost. Theirs was a generous congregation. Within two years the cash was found, the result of many sales of work and concerts, not to mention direct giving by those who could afford.

The necessary consents were obtained from the Local Authority. Then it was all go.

The builders asked the adjoining proprietor to the east for access to his premises for the demolition and rebuilding of the east wall.

He refused.

The contiguous building was an old warehouse, which had been bought speculatively by an estate agent, and held by him empty for several years. Probably waiting for the market to improve – but possibly in the hope he could improve his prospects by acquiring the Kirk Hall too. He knew it was dilapidated. If he could block development it might fall into his hands for a song.

The lawyer was brought in. What did the titles say?

The titles said the brick wall was built wholly on church property, on the line of the boundary. There was no right of access for maintenance. It was impossible to rebuild, so it was thought, without erecting external scaffolding. The neighbour would not permit.

The lawyer was bad news.

What about trying to negotiate with agent a price for very temporary use of a strip of his land, to hold spoiling and scaffolding? His west wall was a good five feet inside their boundary. It would be no skin off his nose. Answer – "No. not at any price." There could be no more sign of transparent bad faith, and bad citizenship. That reinforced the view already expressed, that he gazed with envious eyes. He did not bargain for the versatility of the Deacons' court. The court met on site with the builder. The builder was game.

He demolished the wall, bringing all the spoil down on the church side. He prepared the found, and commenced building from the church side. The rough casting to the new wall was carried out by leaning over the new wall as it rose. Not a foot was placed beyond the line of the old wall.

Three feet up, and lean; three feet up, and lean.

I went to have a look at the work in progress. The builder's men knew all about the problem with the neighbour. Never before did they carry out a similar task. They were keen as mustard to make a good job of their unusual project, laughing their way through it, and giving unchurchman like signs to angry faces appearing to the east. Could be that not always did wise men come out of the east? It did my heart good. I expected that at least there would be a claim for clearance of the small amount of spoil deposited in enemy territory. It did not materialise.

In fear of red faces?

You're a brick.

THE HOMEWRECKER

It was a nice wee house, and I sold it for Altonhead at a good price.

He asked me what the price included, and I said all fixtures, that is anything permanently attached to the fabric of the building, or the garden ground outside.

"But not anything attached by screws?"

"No, but I'd expect you to be reasonable about that."

So the price was paid by the other agents, and the keys were delivered.

Almost immediately the purchaser's agent came on the phone. Altonhead removed all light bulbs, shades and sockets, curtain rails, the sunken door mat, concrete slabs which formed a garden pathway, garden shrubs, and the revolving clothes line.

There was anger. He agreed that on a strict construction, Altonhead was entitled, but at least he could have forewarned the purchaser.

I was livid. I never thought my client could be so evil.

I paid over my conveyancing fee to the purchaser in compensation, without, of course, any admission of liability on my or my client's part.

Never again did I allow a similar situation to arise.

Altonhead was dismissed to find another lawyer.

THE FACTOR AND THE WEDDING

Graham the Farm Manager phoned. A taciturn chap, who loved and understood, so well, his sheep and his sheep dogs.

He was not a great talker. I thought he must keep his talk for his animals.

But we had an excellent relationship, helped, I may say by the excellent results the annual accounts showed. They were pleasing to the Factor, whom was allowed to plough back into the farm and the estate improvements, any profits Graham generated.

The purpose of the phone call was to ask a favour. He had never asked a favour before. His son and his prospective daughter-in-law had made a booking with the Denbroth Hotel, for their wedding reception which was to be on a Saturday five days hence. The hotel told them, sorry, they had double booked, and had to pull out of the arrangement. Would I allow the use of the dining room in the Lodge, the big house, to save the young couple from disaster?

My rapid thoughts were – the laird is not in residence. Graham is an employee regarded with great favour. He and his wife will ensure no damage will be done. And his wife will clean up afterwards to make the room like a new pin.

So my answer was – "Yes certainly. I hope it will be a very happy event, and give my best wishes to the happy couple."

Saturday came and went. Tuesday came, and that was the day for the auction mart. Graham had fifty wedders listed for sale, and I knew he would be in town to see then pass the ring and he would give me a call, and he would have a drink in, and only in such circumstances would he expand. The luckpenny is a grand institution.

He came smiling.

We covered the important business – the result of the sale (which as usual was very good) the numbers forward, the neighbouring farmers who didn't achieve anything like Graham's prices. Then I asked the question – "And how did the wedding go?" "Oh, fine, fine," – ruminating pause. "It was just in time. I had a grandson yesterday."

COMING HOME

A lawyer benefits from being a tactition, or plainly an organiser.

When a prominent Invernessian died in April 1948 in the Barbados, leaving instructions to be buried in Inverness, a long and tortuous journey confronted.

But, strangely, the situation becomes one in which all involved co-operate in full measure.

Cables flashed. The British Consul said that clearance had been granted. He would ship to Greenock, the nearest convenient port. The remains would be embalmed and encased ibn a suitable casket. Who would be the consignee? To whom would expenses be charged?

The consignee would be the lawyers, care of the Greenock undertaker. Accounts to be sent to the lawyers.

The Department of Health in Scotland required no formalities but referred to Customs. Customs in Inverness alerted their counterparts in Greenock. Greenock met with the undertaker there, and accelerated entry, as soon as the ship had docked. The Greenock undertaker travelled north with the coffin, and transferred to the Inverness undertaker.

Meantime arrangements went ahead with the Superintendent at Tomnahurich Cemetery, who was advised of the dimensions of the coffin. The family, and close friends of the family decided on the date and time for the funeral. The Provost and the M.P. were informed. Advertisements were inserted in local and national newspapers. Accommodation was reserved in the Palace Hotel for those who had to travel.

The remains were rested in the West Church for a service presided over by the Rev. Mr Boyd, and the Rev Mr. Grant, on 6th August 1948.

The journey ended near the top of Tomnahurich Hill, in his home town.

The mourners dispersed, having paid their final respects to Matheson Lang.

A RENOWNED TOWNSMAN

As a youngster Matheson Lang caught the thesbian bug, to the extent of constructing a stage, in the Manse to act out plays with his elder brother. His father, the Rev. Gavin Lang, Minister of the West Parish Church, frowned upon these activities. Resisting parental pressure, the young Matheson spent his every penny to take seats in the Gods at the local Theatre Royal. Flouting pressure, and still in his teens, he succeeded in persuading a London producer to give him "bit" parts. Presaging his destiny, he had the effrontery to book the Theatre Royal for a week to show the Merchant of Venice, in which he played Shylock. He brought some of his very young theatrical friends north from London to help. The costumes were lost in transit, and sat in Waverley Station, while the players continued in evening dress. Inverness was not impressed. He said himself he didn't set the Ness on fire.

His monumental success was as the Wandering Jew. For a year it played in London, once before King George V and his Queen Mary, for charity. He brought it to Inverness in October 1936, and played in the Empire Theatre. If he sought to conquer Inverness he did it then. His was a masterful portrayal of the erring Jew, who spurned Christ, and was condemned to wander the world will the day of Judgement. Theatre goers had the choice of paying for seats – 5/-, 3/6d., 2/6d., or 1/-.

Faith in Jud Suss, written by Dr. Lion Feuchtwanger in 1925, was illustrated by Lang's acquisition of all rights in 1927.

He conceivably became the greatest dramatic actor in Britain in the period between the wars.

Here are some of Mr. Lang's successes:-

> Plays:
> > Mr. Wu.
> > The Bad Man.
> > The Tyrant.
> > Such Men are dangerous.
> > The Wandering Jew.
> > The Private Secretary.
> > She Stoops to Conquer.
> > John Storm.
> > Much Ado About Nothing.
> > The Merchant of Venice.

> Films:

shown in Inverness
> > Duck Turpin's Ride to York.
> > Carnival.
> > Wandering Jew.
> > Guy Fawkes.
> > Jealousy.
> > Henry King of Navarre.
> > Slaves of Destiny.
> > White Slippers.
> > The Qualified Adventurer.
> > The Chinese Bungalow.
> > Island of Despair.
> > The Chinese Bungalow – his first Talkie in 1930

In the annals of British Theatre there will be for ever a salute for a wee Inverness boy, stage struck.